The *Last* Shall Be First, and the *First* Shall Be Last

The Diary of a First Lady

Maretha Johnican

ISBN 979-8-88943-927-1 (paperback)
ISBN 979-8-88943-928-8 (digital)

Christian Faith Publishing
832 Park Avenue
Meadville, PA 16335
www.christianfaithpublishing.com

Printed in the United States of America

Chapter 1

ONE OF MY EARLIEST MEMORIES WAS BEING transported to the hospital in an ambulance one night, with the sirens squealing and the bright lights flashing. It was a rough ride as the ambulance sped along the city streets. It was a very frightening experience for a child of two or three years old.

I was fighting to get my breath as the strange paramedics worked on me. We would come to know that I had asthma. We would also come to know that these asthma attacks were triggered by a variety of things, including stress, fear, anxiety, climate change, and overexertion.

My parents had been fighting that night, which was a routine occurrence in our run-down home in the projects of Cleveland, Ohio. If my parents agreed on anything, it was truly a miracle. During this episode, I got so upset, while they were fussing and fighting, that it sent me to the emergency room.

My older brother and I were only thirteen months apart in age. We were close in age, and our relationship would also grow to be very close over the years. We would share our deepest thoughts and dreams with one another. We would also share the same fears, insecurities, and uncertainties, as we grew up in our violently charged, chaotic home.

Our parents not only fought verbally, but they also fought physically. My father was around six-foot tall, and my mother was around five-foot tall. It was very traumatic to see my father's huge hands balled into a fist, punching away at my mother's head and face. But she would not back down for anything. If he wanted a fight, she would give him one.

On one occasion, she was getting ready to go to an after-school event with me, and he came home. He had been drinking, as was his almost daily routine. He asked her where she was going, and she told him. He forbade her to go, but she was determined to do so. The fight quickly escalated, and I saw my father black both of my mother's eyes that night. One of my mother's eyes was swollen completely shut with a cut over it.

The violence would continue for several years. Sometimes the neighbors would call the police. We would hear the officers warn her to leave him before he killed her. The laws concerning domestic violence were a lot different back in the early sixties. He was rarely arrested.

At times, we would move to get away from him, only for him to eventually find out where we had moved to. He would beg my mother for forgiveness, and she would end up taking him back. But it was only a short period of time before the violence and his other bad habits start up again.

My father was not only violent with my mother, but he would get into brawls with other people. I remember him starting a fight with a man because he owed him a quarter, a dollar, or some small amount of money. Once someone got the best of him, and he ended up with a broken jaw. He had to have it wired shut. He was also in and out of jail for one form of misconduct or another.

My father had been in the Vietnam War. He obviously had been extremely traumatized during his tour of duty. There were times when he would line my mother, my brother, and I up as if we were on a firing line. He would hold us at gunpoint, cursing and threatening to kill us. Once he pulled the trigger, and a bullet just missed my mother's foot; it ricocheted off the floor and went into the ceiling.

Another time, he held us hostage in the bathroom and played cat and mouse with us throughout the night. My mother sat on the toilet seat by the door all night long as if to protect us. She had my brother and I lie down in the tub. My father would go away for random periods of time, and then he would come back and start to bang loudly on the door, cursing and screaming and threatening to kill us.

Chapter 2

BOTH OF OUR PARENTS HAD GROWN UP in Christian homes in the country. My paternal grandfather was a minister in Alabama. My maternal grandparents lived in North Carolina and then moved to West Virginia. I heard stories about how my maternal grandparents used to party, but they had become Christians quite a few years before my mother left home. I was told that my mother had been saved and would praise the Lord openly in church. Both of our parents had moved to the big city of Cleveland and met and married there.

Occasionally, my mother or father would take us to church, but usually not together as a family. My father had been called to preach. He could preach, pray better drunk than most preachers could sober. He also had a beautiful singing voice and had been in a men's a cappella gospel singing group for a while. But unfortunately, my father would never walk in his calling due to his strong addiction to wine, women, and song.

It was after one of those rare times of going to church that I felt, saw, and heard God's presence in my bedroom. I was making my bed and trying to sing a song that I had heard in church. Suddenly, I saw a bright light come into my room, and I felt the loving arms of God encircle me in the warmest embrace I had ever experienced. The Lord told me that things would not always be this way, and that everything was going to be alright. I would hear Him speak these very words to me many times throughout my childhood and adult life.

Chapter 3

Papa was a rolling stone. Oftentimes, Daddy would take my brother and me along with him on his escapades. It was not unusual for us to end up in a bar, where he would have us dance for money. However, he would take the money for himself after we left the bar.

At other times, we might end up at one of his family member's or associate's houses where he would gamble the evening and half the night away. My brother and I would have long since fallen asleep over on a chair or couch, after he had fed us potato chips and sodas for supper. He would finally wake us up and take us home, sometimes in the wee hours of the morning. I'm sure my mother must have been worried about where we were and if we were okay.

My father was a ladies' man. He was tall, medium brown, and handsome. He dressed to impress. He had wavy black hair and a smile that would dazzle the women. There were times when he would take my brother and I to one of his various female friend's homes and leave us sitting in the living room for hours watching television, while they stole away to another part of the house.

My father worked jobs that had pretty good pay in the 1960s and early '70s. I remember him working for Republic Steel and

Central Cadillac. He always drove one of the newest, fanciest cars, usually a Cadillac.

However, he was not a good provider. He would oftentimes have just gotten paid and know that there was no food in the house, but he would not buy any groceries. Occasionally, he would bring something home for us to eat. Sometimes he might cook, but he would put so much black pepper in the food, we could not eat it. There were many times when we did not know where our next meal was coming from.

My father always seemed to keep a lot of change in his pockets. Oftentimes, he would collapse on the couch after he had drunk himself into a stupor. On several occasions, my mother would check under the pillows on the couch and find enough change to buy us something to eat, after he had gotten up and left the house.

Chapter 4

MY MOTHER WORKED PART-TIME FOR SOME OF the "rich folks" in Shaker Heights, Ohio. She would clean, cook, or whatever they desired her to do. But she did not make very much money doing that type of work, and it would take her quite a while to get to work and back using the rapids or buses for her transportation.

My mother taught us the importance of getting an education. I loved it when she read to us and told us stories. She taught my brother and I how to read and write before we started public school. However, my mother was oftentimes stressed out and angry, which is not surprising considering the situation in which we lived. Unfortunately, she would oftentimes take her frustration out on us kids. It was not unusual for us to get yelled at, cursed out, and spanked for little of nothing.

My mother decided to start going to school to become a licensed practical nurse, to make a better living for us. My fate was sealed for wanting to become a nurse when I was five years old. It was something that really appealed to me seeing her class graduation picture with all the nursing students dressed in their white caps, starched white uniforms, and white stockings and shoes.

Oftentimes, my brother and I had to stay at home by ourselves for long hours, until our mother came home from work or school. My father would never take the responsibility of watching us, whether he could or not. He would only have us with him when it was convenient for him.

My brother and I truly felt free when we could go out outside and play. We would race, climb trees, jump off high walls, wrestle, or whatever else we could find to do. I was a pure tomboy. I believed that I could do whatever my brother did. He still admits to this day that I could climb trees better than he could.

Sometimes, it would be him and me and a few of the neighborhood boys who would play together. My brother was very outgoing and made friends easily. Sometimes, I would watch in amazement as he would strike up conversations with anyone, adults as well as children. I, on the other hand, did not make friends as easily. I was nice, but I tended to be somewhat apprehensive and shy. So I preferred to play with him and his friends, rather than venture out to find my own friends.

Chapter 5

ONE DAY WHEN I WAS FIVE YEARS old, our fifteen-year-old cousin came to visit. My mother let my brother and I go out to play, and he went with us. We got with our some of our little neighborhood friends and decided to go to the wooded area not far from our home. We called this area our *secret hideout*. We started playing hide and seek, as we often did.

During one of the hiding and seeking pursuits, when our cousin was "it," he grabbed me just as we were getting ready to run and find our hiding places. The others continued to run, but he pulled me into an area of the woods, and he proceeded to pull down my pants and expose himself. He sat me on his on his lap and was attempting to penetrate, when one of the smaller boys wandered to where we were and stood there watching. My cousin tried to make him go away, but he just stood there. This made my cousin uncomfortable, and he discontinued his attempt to rape me.

I knew that what happened was wrong, but I was too afraid to say something about it when we got home. However, the little boy followed us home and told my mother about what he had seen, to the best of his ability. He could only have been two or three years old. However, she was able to figure out for the most part what he was trying to tell her.

My mother started yelling at me and ordered me to go upstairs to my room. She left me there wondering what I had done wrong, for what seemed to be an eternity. I cannot remember what she said to me after that, but it left an imprint in my mind that it was my fault. I was no longer permitted to play with my brother and his friends outside. My innocence had been shattered, and I was deprived of the fun I had previously had with my brother and our friends. It was the beginning of my long road of guilt, shame, condemnation, loneliness, and undiagnosed recurring depression.

Chapter 6

My mother got a job at Case Western Reserve Hospital. At five and six years old, my brother and I would have to get ourselves ready for school, after our mother had left for work. My mother would set the alarm for us to get up. She gave us keys to the apartment so we could lock the door when we left for school and let ourselves in after school.

The school was too far for children our age to have to walk by ourselves. But we had to do what we had to do. We walked ourselves to and from school in the sun, rain, sleet, or snow. I had a weak bladder, as my mother called it, and sometimes I would wet my clothes before we made it home. Some days, I would get so cold that I would be crying by the time we finally got home. My mother would not get home until after dark, especially during the winter months.

I can remember being made fun of because my hair was a mess or my clothes were too small or big or wrinkled. However, I did make a few friends at school, but I always felt like I was *the last* among them. Their hair was always combed neatly, and they had the latest styles in clothes. We would usually get clothes when they were going out of style. I felt ugly and inferior to them.

My feelings were confirmed, when the most popular boy in class was asked by some of my friends whom he liked. He chose all my friends, but he did not choose me. I felt like going and crawling under a rock someplace. The spirit of rejection would creep in and have his way with me for many years.

Over the next few years, my father and mother would break up and get back together many times, and the violence would start soon afterward. My mother had three more children after my older brother and me. My sister was born when I was four and a half years old; another brother was born a little over two years after her; and my youngest brother almost two years after him.

The responsibilities for my older brother and I continued to increase as each additional child was born. We had to grow up fast. Before my brother and I were able to read, my mother would send us to the neighborhood grocery store. We had to cross a huge street, with several lanes of traffic, to get there. However, my mother had taken us to the store several times before and had taught us how to cross the street safely. Oftentimes, she would draw pictures of the food she was sending us to purchase. Like little cans with peas on the label, etc. Sometimes we did not get it right. I can remember bringing home lettuce instead of cabbage.

Sometimes, my older brother would be allowed to go out to play, but oftentimes I would have to stay in and care for my younger sister and brothers, since I was the oldest girl. And of course, I was not permitted to play with my brother and his friends anymore.

I remember having to stand on a chair to wash dishes. I boiled bottles and prepared milk for my younger siblings. I gave baths and combed hair. I washed poop out of cloth diapers in the toilet before they could be washed in a washing machine. Oftentimes, I felt like I was being punished for being a girl.

My mom would sometimes refer to my older brother and me as our siblings' second set of parents, or "the big guys." We were the built-in babysitters, and nothing could go wrong while my mother was gone, or else we would get into big trouble. Oftentimes, we were too young to understand what we were doing, but we learned to follow instructions very closely.

Chapter 7

OVER THE NEXT FEW YEARS, MY FATHER's behavior only grew worse. We were living in the last apartment that the family would share with my father. My older brother and I had gotten to be about seven and eight years old. Our father had started hanging out getting drunk at a bar that we passed as we walked to and from school.

One morning, there was a big group of us kids walking to school, and I saw my father up ahead in front of the bar, passing out money to some of the kids. I hid myself in the crowd and made sure that he did not see me. I did not know what he might say or do to embarrass us.

I can remember to this day how insignificant I felt seeing my father giving money to children he did not know, while his own family's cupboards were bare.

Once he had seen my brother and I walking past the bar, he came out sloppy drunk and had us escort him home. It was really embarrassing, because at least a couple of our classmates saw us, as he held onto us staggering along. He had one of us on one side of him and one on the other, almost pulling us to the ground at times. We were much too small to try and hold him up.

Some of the children started making fun of us after they realized that he was our father. Apparently, someone had even seen him fall over into some bushes as he was heading home drunk one day.

It was nothing for him to be singing church songs or preaching at the top of his voice as he was heading home drunk. Sometimes, we could hear him way up the street before he got home. Other times, he would be cursing and hurling insults at our mother, such as, you old spotted cow or spotted leopard.

My mother had a rare skin condition that years later we found out was called vitiligo. The pigmentation of her skin was gradually fading. My mother was dark-brown skinned, and the faded areas were very white. It was like that all over her body. For years, she would buy make up and try to cover up the white areas on her face. Sometimes, she could blend the make up over the lightened areas, and it looked pretty good, but other times the makeup made it look worse.

Some people would laugh and make fun of her, while others would act as if her condition was contagious, and still others were bold enough to ask her what was wrong with her. At times she would explain, and at other times her response was not too friendly. I guess it depended on the way they approached her or what mood she was in.

Once my mother had a birthday party for me at our apartment, and she told me I could invite some of my friends. When they came, some of them acted as if there was nothing different about my mother, but there were a couple who acted as if they were afraid to eat what she had prepared as if she was poison. I was torn. I loved my mother, and it hurt me to see people treating her this way. But I was also beginning to be embarrassed about people knowing that she was my mother. Why did my mother have to be this way? Why did I have to be born into this messed up family?

Chapter 8

MY MOTHER ENDED UP TAKING OUR THREE younger siblings to my grandparents in West Virginia, as it had become too hard for her to try to fend for all of us in different stages of development. My older brother and I were able to get to and from school and do a lot for ourselves. But our little sister and brothers had to be cared for 24-7.

Also, my mother said our father had tried to kill my youngest brother, by letting him fall off a table when he was about a month old. My father never claimed my baby brother as his child and would call him awful names.

My brother suffered neurological damage from that fall for several years. His neck would draw over to one side, and he would not be unable to lift his head to an upright position. But we had a praying grandmother, and she anointed him with oil and prayed until the Lord healed him.

One day, my father told my older brother and I that we could go out to play. After a while, he called us in and asked us who told us we could go outside. We had to tell him that he did, but that was the wrong thing to say. He called us liars and whipped both of us.

Even though he was physically abusive to our mother, it was very rare that he would spank us. This made my mother very upset.

She realized that what the police officers had been telling her was true; he would eventually begin to abuse us.

After my father left the apartment, my mother took my brother and me to a hotel. It was good to get away from my father for those couple of days. We really had a good time with our mother. I will never forget; we went to see the movie *Ben*, and we talked and laughed like we had not done in quite some time. We hated to go back to the apartment, for fear that our father would be there.

When we got back home, we saw a lot of our furniture on the front lawn soaked with water. We found out later that our father had sporadically set a variety of fires throughout the apartment. He had set fire to our bunk beds, our living room suit, and other items in the apartment. Someone had apparently smelled or seen the smoke and called the fire department. Thank God, most of the furniture was salvageable.

Of course, my father said he had discovered the fire and had tried to put it out. My father lied so much that it seemed like he convinced himself of a lot of them. My mother called him an unmitigated liar.

One Sunday morning, after gambling all night, he took my brother and I straight from the gambling house to church. We looked awful. My father stood up in church and announced that his wife and other children had been killed in a car accident, and he needed money to bury them. They took up a collection for him.

One beautiful spring day, my father came home drunk. He began to beat on my mother and threatened to kill us, as he had often done before. My mother had suffered concussions, black eyes, lumps, bruises, and only God knows what else by his hands and feet. But this time, he would come as close to killing her as I had ever known.

My father pulled out a straight razor. The fight progressed outdoors, as she tried to get away from him. My brother and I came out of the apartment right behind them. We did not want him to kill our mother. He raised the hand holding the straight razor and went for my mother's throat. She put up her arm up just in time to prevent the blade from slicing her throat, but it sliced down into her forearm instead. We saw the flesh of her forearm peel open like an overcooked sausage link. He had cut to the bone. Blood was gushing everywhere. My mother screamed to my brother and me and told us to run for our lives.

We did not want to leave our mother standing there wounded and bleeding. We heard the sirens and saw the rescue squad pulling up (she would be safe). My father started to leave the scene in the direction that we were standing. We could run now. We ran hard and fast, making sure that he did not catch up to us.

Once we realized we were well out of his reach, we finally stopped running. We wondered where we should go. We decided to go back to a woman's apartment who lived in the apartment building across from ours. My mother had told us to go there in case of an emergency; and this was certainly an emergency.

When we arrived, the lady told us that she was glad we came. My mother was able to call her from the hospital and let us know that she would be okay. We stayed there until my mother was treated and released to come home the next day.

My mother ended up having to get layers of sutures in her arm, and she had to go and hold her arm under an ultraviolet light so many times a week, for healing purposes. Her arm finally healed, but she would continue to complain of numbness and pain in that arm for years to come.

We found out that our father had been apprehended and arrested for the assault. I think he stayed in jail for about a month. Things had gotten pretty much back to our normal, without him around.

One day, when my mother was at work and my brother and I were home alone, we heard a loud knock at the front door. We looked through the peephole and saw that it was our father. We panicked and hurried and ran out of the back door. When the coast was clear, we ended up going back to the same lady's apartment who lived across from us. She was able to get in touch with my mother and let her know what had happened.

Once again, we went to say in a hotel room to stay safe. But this time, my mother finally made up her mind to get away from my father for good.

I loved my father, but I was terrified of him. I wished our lives could be normal and that we could be a loving family. But that just was not going to happen.

Chapter 9

MY MOTHER TOOK MY BROTHER AND I to West Virginia after the school year was over, and we were joined with our younger brothers and sister at our grandparents' home. I was my grandparents' first granddaughter. My mother went back to Cleveland for a while.

My grandparents had a son and daughter who were older than we were, but they were still in school. Our aunt was in elementary school, and our uncle was in junior high school. Their other children, including my mother, had grown up and left home.

It was like culture shock to move from the city to the country. Even though we lived in poverty in the city, we were used to having electric heat, hot water from the faucet, and a bathtub in the bathroom.

We had to get accustomed to getting warmed by a coal stove and heating water for baths, dishwashing, and other uses on the coal stove. We learned that to take a bath, we had to bring the big aluminum wash tub into the house and fill it with heated water before getting into it.

We also had to get accustomed to chickens running around in the yard, slopping hogs, and helping to tend to a huge vegetable garden that my grandmother raised across the railroad tracks. We learned how to bring in coal and wood and make fires in the coal stoves.

We were free from the violence and abuse we had been subjected to in Cleveland. And even though it was hard work, we found peace, for a while anyway.

We had fun during our first summer there. Us younger kids were not allowed to go very far, but it was fun just being able to play in the yard or on the dirt road right in front of the house. On occasion, we were permitted to go up or down the road a little way to play with some of the other children in the neighborhood, but we always had to go in when the streetlights came on.

The relocation was just what we needed, except for the fact that one of our family members had started to molest me during the summer. I was afraid to tell anyone for fear that I would get into trouble. Once again, I thought it must be my fault. The self-worth that I had started to regain was quickly extinguished.

After the summer was over, it was time to go back to school. I loved school as I always had. But it was not long before the children started to single my older brother and me out as the outsiders. We were from the city, and we talked differently and had some mannerisms that were different.

The children would make fun of us and call us names. At times, things would escalate, and we were provoked into fighting. I started to dread going to school for fear of what they would say or do the next day.

Chapter 10

M Y MOTHER MOVED DOWN FROM CLEVELAND DURING the winter of the first school year. We moved into my grandparents'
previous house that was right across the dirt road from where they
were living at the time.

We were happy to be reunited with our mother. But it would
not take long for her anger to start to flare up again. We would get
spankings sometimes, because she was having a bad day. Sometimes
we were beaten with a belt or switch, and sometimes with an exten-
sion cord. I can remember my oldest brother having a sore on his leg
that got infected and took weeks to heal, from one of those beatings.
My sister bore a scar beneath one of her ears that remained there for
years.

My mother eventually found out about how the kids were treating us. My brother came home one day with one whole side of his
face enormously swollen, from one of the kids hitting him with a
rock. My mother had it out with at least a couple of the parents, but
it just made things worse. It was as if the kids and their parents were
against us then.

The kids started to make fun of our mother as well. Her pigmentation was still fading. They started up where the people in
Cleveland had left off, with a vengeance.

They also made fun of us because of our living situation as we were still living in poverty. Our clothes were oftentimes too large or small and out of style. The house that we moved into was in dire need of a paint job, and certain areas were in desperate need of repair. We were one of the last in the community to still have an outside toilet.

The neighbors did not know that we never had hot water while we lived in that house. We had to heat water to wash ourselves, or whatever else we needed hot water for. That would have been one more thing that they could have made fun of us about.

All five of us kids slept in bunk beds in the one big bedroom upstairs. My mother made a place for herself downstairs in the living room. The only other room that was partially usable was the kitchen, but one side of the floor was caving in and allowed rats and mice to easily go in and out. One day, some of the old men who used to hang out at a house near ours saw a rat drag a partial loaf of bread out of our house. That was their laugh for the day, and even days to come.

I tried to be grateful for what we had, but it was hard sometimes. The Lord would oftentimes comfort me by telling me that it would not always be this way. These words continued to soothe my troubled mind many nights as I lay awake in bed, tossing and turning. I did not know what depression was, but as I look back, I realize that I was a depressed child.

My depression made me feel hopeless and helpless. I lacked confidence and quickly gave up on things. For example, when I was in the fifth or sixth grade, I deliberately misspelled a word in a spelling bee so that I would not be chosen to go to the regional spelling bee to represent our school. The contest had gotten down to me and one other student. I began to panic, not because I was afraid of losing—I was afraid of winning. I could spell above my grade level, but I was so timid and insecure that I could not imagine being chosen for anything as important as this.

I would even give up on things at home. If my brother was winning against me while we were playing a board game and started teasing me, I would quit.

I would start working on arts and crafts that my mother had bought me, but it was not long before I would lose interest and quit.

My mother would oftentimes call me a quitter or a loser. I realized it was true, even though I hated to hear her refer to me in this way. But somewhere deep inside, I promised myself that it wouldn't always be this way.

Chapter 11

WE WERE ON WELFARE FOR QUITE SOME time until my mother could find a job and get transportation. It was difficult for her to accomplish either one. We lived in a place called McDowell (way up in Northfork Hollow). It was quite a way to the nearest small city and even further to one of the hospitals or nursing homes. My mother's first nursing job was at least an hour away.

Our mother worked for the remainder of the time I was still at home. But she had to provide for five children, and sometimes she would splurge and buy things that were not needed at the time. We were no strangers to having the lights or telephone disconnected for lack of payment. Once our lights were turned off for over a month, and we had to use candles and kerosene lamps when it got dark. We also saw the repo guys come and take a car out of our driveway; while my mother cursed and threatened, trying to intimidate them from doing so.

When my mother started working, she started to meet more people. Before long, she started to date. My mother and father never got divorced, but thank God, they never got back together. However, we would see our father from time to time throughout the years.

Once, my mother received a call from someone who told her that my father had been killed in a car accident. My mother packed up all of us kids and went to Cleveland just to find out that it was not true. My father said he was almost killed in the car accident. He acted as if he could hardly walk and even called on us kids to help him get out of his chair. However, my mother said she saw him get up and walk without any problem when he thought we were all sleep.

I guess my father just wanted to see us. At least he did give our mother money to get us all a couple of new outfits during the trip. However, he never paid child support. We stayed a few days and headed back home.

My older brother and I were oftentimes confined to the house babysitting from sunup to sundown due to our mother going to visit with one of her beaus all day during the weekend. We were not permitted to go outside if she was not home.

Our grandmother would rescue us sometimes, to take us to church with her. I enjoyed it because it got us out of the house and allowed us to be with her and around other people.

She did not drive, so during the summer months, there were times when we walked to church for Wednesday night Bible study. It had to be at least three miles from where we lived. But we would always get a ride home with one of the members. She was determined to get to church, whether it meant walking or paying someone to take us. Our grandfather drove, but he was not home much, and at the time, he was not going to church.

Our grandmother was a devoted missionary in the church. We would oftentimes go with her and the other women in their prayer band, especially us girls. We would go to see people who were sick in their homes, in the hospitals, and nursing homes. These people were unable to come to church, so they took the church to them.

I was baptized at the age of nine, after a revival that lasted a week or two. My aunt who was only a couple of years older than me was also baptized. I partially understood what I was doing and wanted a closer relationship with the Lord. However, the picture that was oftentimes painted of Him was that of a strict disciplinarian, who was always eager to punish when we messed up.

The years of going to church with my grandmother had a positive impact on my life, especially in my later years. As the Bible says, "Train up a child in the way he should go and when he is old, he will not depart from it" (Proverbs 22:6).

Chapter 12

THINGS SEEMED TO GET A LITTLE BETTER when I started going to junior high school. It seemed as if the children in our neighborhood had more interesting things to do than to pick on us full-time. I was also able to make a few friends at our new school. But the poverty and molestation continued.

I was also exposed to pornography at a very young age. One day, when my mother was away and I was cleaning up, I discovered some magazines that she had tucked out of sight. I knew I should not be looking at them, but I just could not seem to put them down. I would oftentimes sneak and look at them when she was not home. This led to years of an addiction to pornography and masturbation. Talking about adding insult to injury. My self-esteem continued to plummet. I was very self-conscience, shy, guilt-ridden, and felt that I had no self-worth or value. I even wondered sometimes, *Why am I here?* or *Why was I ever born?*

Despite of how I saw myself, the boys started to notice me. I would drop my head, to avoid eye contact with them. I had a few so-called boyfriends, but the relationships did not last very long.

I did not feel like I deserved the "nice boys" who asked to go steady with me, so I would find a way to sabotage the relationships. The guilt and shame that I carried made me feel like I only deserved the "bad boys." I yearned for healthy relationships, but I was too broken to establish any.

I began a pattern of settling and looking for love in all the wrong places. I subconsciously looked for guys who were just as broken, or even more broken than myself.

The molestation continued throughout my teenage years. I never initiated the episodes, but I did not stop them either. I did not want my perpetrator to get mad at me, and in some perverted way, I welcomed the attention. I felt unwanted and rejected when he seemed to ignore me and did not approach me.

My soul was in bondage. I was torn and broken. I hated the feelings of guilt, shame, and worthlessness, but somehow it gave me a sense of being wanted or needed. I had a dirty little secret that was destroying whom God created me to be.

Chapter 13

I REMEMBER IT LIKE IT WAS YESTERDAY; I was fifteen years old and a sophomore in high school. One night, we went to a revival service at another church. It happened during the praise and worship portion of the service when the Spirit was high.

Suddenly, one of the choir members came down out of the choir stand and began to circle the church. She had circled one side of the church and was heading down the center aisle, when she suddenly stopped by the pew where I was seated.

She looked me in my eyes and began to prophesy to me, telling me about my future. She warned me that Satan had traps lain for me and was plotting to destroy my life at a young age. I cannot remember her exact words, but she compelled me to give my life to the Lord before it was too late.

I was really shaken up and frightened by the prophecy. I was one of the first ones to go to the altar when the altar call was made by the preacher. I repented and asked the Lord to save me, with tears running down my face. From the time I first started learning about God, there was a part of me that wanted to please and obey Him. But it did not take long for the distractions of this world to start taking precedence over what I knew to be right.

I soon began to yield to the temptations that were ever-present. Granted, the children in our family led a sheltered life, but I took advantage of any opportunities that arose. However, I knew more than ever that God had His hand on me. I could hear the convictions of the Holy Spirit, and I could never really enjoy the sins that I committed—although I tried!

A few short months after the prophecy, my life began to spin out of control. I started to shed the outward layer of the quiet, shy, self-conscious people pleaser. I began to transform into a wild, rebellious, promiscuous chance taker. I convinced myself to believe that I did not care about what happened in my life anymore or what people thought about me.

I wanted to break out of the box that I felt others had put me in. I was tired of being used to care for my younger brothers and sister and believed I was not appreciated. Satan convinced me that instead of being molested at someone else's will that I should chose whom I would sleep with. I gave the enemy an inch, and he took a mile. I let him ride, and he started to drive.

I wanted to be like some of the other girls who could go where they wanted to go and do what they wanted to do, even though some of them had gotten pregnant in junior high school and had bad reputations before they ever reached high school. I did not realize at the time that being sheltered was a blessing.

An opportunity arose in the spring of that year. My aunt was a senior in high school, soon to graduate, and I was a sophomore. We were allowed to go to a concert with my uncle and his wife. We all had been drinking alcohol and smoking weed on the way to the concert, and I had a serious buzz.

I had a boyfriend, but I had found out some time before that, he had cheated on me, and I was still somewhat bitter about it. During the concert, I was approached by one of the high schools "bad boys." He was always being taken to the principal's office for fighting or something or other. Even though I was high, I knew I did not need to get involved with him. He was a girl chaser and had been known to physically abuse his girlfriends, but it was an opportunity after all! I did not want to go back home without getting into something that

I should not. Who knows when I would have gotten another opportunity? When I look back, I see how mixed up I was!

He asked me to go outside with him, and well, you know the rest. I did not want to make anything out of what happened. I guess I looked at it as a one-night stand. I thought we would forget that it ever happened and move ahead. But that Monday at school, he came looking for me and proceeded to try to establish a relationship.

I really did not like him; he was not my type. But what was my type? I did not know how to say no. I did not know what to do. I had gotten myself into something that was easy to get into, but getting out would leave me even more scarred and broken!

My two-year relationship with my boyfriend was history. Even though he had cheated, he was a nice guy for the most part. He was very smart and was never in any serious trouble. We had never been intimate. I felt that I really cared for him and had even thought that one day we might be married. I really felt bad about how our relationship ended so abruptly!

The "bad boy" started to follow me around in the halls between classes and calling me when we got out of school. He would also come to visit me, with one of the other high school boys who came to visit my aunt. I started a vicious cycle of bad relationships that I would not find myself getting out of for years to come.

Chapter 14

MY AUNT GRADUATED THAT YEAR AND DID not waste any time leaving home. She had said for some time that she was leaving home as soon as she graduated, and she was not kidding! She went to live with one of my aunts (her sister) in New York. But before she left, my grandmother had us paint the room that we slept in. While we were painting, I suddenly found myself getting dizzy and nauseated; I had to sit down for quite some time before I could go back to work.

That day wasn't the only day that I would get dizzy and nauseated. My grandfather told me a while later that I was pregnant, but I denied the possibility.

During the first part of the summer, my mother took me to the hospital, and it was confirmed that I was pregnant. I was sixteen years old. My grandmother did not say much before I got tested, but afterward, she said she knew I was pregnant when I got sick while we were painting.

The "bad boy" had continued to call and visit, and now I had to tell him that we were pregnant. Now that I was pregnant, the damage had been done, and I was allowed to go on outings with him when he could borrow his father's truck.

He asked me to marry him. I was not expecting that. I really do not know what I was expecting. Even though I was pregnant, I did not want to get married. I was too young. We were only going to be juniors in high school. I was not in love with him. I was in a state of confusion. What had I done?

My grandmother attempted to shame me into accepting the proposal, by telling me that I had brought disgrace to the family, and I needed to go ahead and get married. I explained that I was not in love with him, but she did not seem to care about that. It seemed like she judged me even more when I told her that, especially since he was really playing the part of the devoted father-to-be.

My mother offered to assist me with getting an abortion, but as young as I was, I could not see killing the baby. I would just have to deal with the situation that I had created, even if it took me the next eighteen years. One thing that having to care for my younger brothers and sisters had taught me was to be responsible, even when I made bad mistakes.

The summer moved ahead, and we were still seeing each other. He was still talking about getting married. He was seventeen years old and wanted to get married after his eighteenth birthday in October. He seemed to be growing on my grandparents and mother. They seemed to like him. I met his parents that summer, and they treated me nicely as well. But everyone knew that we were too young to be in the situation that we were in.

I was about three months pregnant and was beginning to show a little. One Sunday morning, I got up and went to the bathroom. I had experienced some mild cramping and felt something come out of me. When I looked down, I saw the baby hanging there. It looked like a "beet red" Barbie doll.

I could see the fetus from the shoulders down. It had come out feet first. I stayed there in the bathroom for quite some time, just trying to digest what was going on. I saw two legs and counted the five miniature toes on each perfectly formed foot. I counted the five miniature fingers on one perfectly formed hand. However, the other hand had never developed; it was just a portion of an arm there. I believe that the lead in the paint had caused the baby to be deformed, and it eventually led to me having a miscarriage.

I tried to finish pulling the baby out, but it caused excruciating pain when I tried to do so. I finally called for my uncle's wife to come into the bathroom where I was to show her what had happened. My grandparents were not at home; they had gone to church. My uncle and his wife took me to the hospital. We called my mother and let her know what had happened, and she met us at the hospital. They pumped my stomach and performed a D&C. I stayed in the hospital for a couple of days.

My boyfriend did not come to visit me in the hospital, but he came to see me when I got home. By now he had started to grow on me a little more. I had started to be quite fond of him.

Chapter 15

IT WAS SOMEWHAT OF A RELIEF THAT I would not have to raise a baby at my age and still in high school. I knew it would be more difficult for me to concentrate on my studies and graduate while caring for a baby. However, I still went through a period of mourning for this baby that I had felt growing and moving inside me, ever so subtly. But my mother and I made sure I got on birth control pills after that.

My grandmother ended up telling me that she had prayed "that something like this would happen," and that there was no need for me to get married anymore. I really felt some type of way after hearing her say this. How could she pray that my baby would die? Hadn't she had a baby when she was unmarried and sixteen years old, even though she did not talk about it? As a matter of fact, that baby was my mother. I also felt like she had been willing to "throw me to the wolves," when she told me I needed to marry him, even after I told her I did not love him. My grandfather added fuel to the fire when he told me that "only a woman could have a baby." I loved my grandparents, and I later came to realize that they had my best interest at heart. But at the time, I became resentful.

I kept in touch with my father by writing letters to him occasionally, whenever I knew his address. I had written and told him I was pregnant a short time after the results were confirmed, without my mother's knowledge. I had not written to him again after I had the miscarriage. To our surprise, he paid us a visit. This was the first time he had come to visit us since he and my mother had separated. He blamed my mother for allowing me to get pregnant. My mother was upset with me for telling him. If I had known I was going to have a miscarriage, I would never have told him. Not much had changed. He and my mother still could not agree on anything.

He went to church with us kids and our grandparents one day. He asked my grandfather to stop at the store on the way. He bought a six pack of beer and proceeded to drink it in the car on the way to church. My grandfather was not too pleased about it, to say the least.

My father only visited a few days before going back to Cleveland.

Chapter 16

STRANGELY ENOUGH, MY BOYFRIEND SAID HE STILL wanted to marry me after I had the miscarriage. I tried to talk him into waiting until after we graduated, to see if we still wanted to get married then, but he would not hear of it. He claimed to love me and wanted to spend the rest of his life with me. Even though I still did not feel that we should get married, I decided that I would marry him anyway; I would show them! Until this day, I really do not know why he was so insistent about getting married. Maybe he was trying to prove something to his parents as well.

His birthday came in October, and we were determined to get married, regardless of what his parents or my mother or grandparents had to say. I wanted to get out of the house and away from them, and I was tired of taking care of children who were not mine. I would later deeply regret making this terrible decision.

My husband-to-be worked part-time at a gas station near his parent's home, and of course, he was not making much money. But he told me that his boss had a house that he was willing to rent to us for little of nothing. I cannot believe I fell for it, but I never even saw the house before we were married.

We had to go to Virginia to get married; after all, I was still a minor, and they did not allow sixteen-year-olds to get married in

West Virginia. But my mother would still have to sign for me to get married in Virginia. She warned me again and again not to go forward with the marriage. But she finally agreed to go to the justice of peace with us and sign the papers for me to get married, after she saw that I was adamant about going through with it. She knew what would happen, but she was kind enough to let me see for myself. My uncle and his wife went along as witnesses.

On our wedding night, we sat outside in the driveway of my husband's parents' home, in his father's truck with nowhere to go. He had previously told me that his employer was going to rent him a house for us to live in when we were married. But he was now explaining that the deal had fallen through, and his boss was working on renting him another house that should be ready to rent out before too long. How naive I was; I had never insisted on seeing the house prior to us getting married.

He went inside to his parents and asked if we could stay there temporarily, but they said no. They said they told him that he was not ready for marriage, just as my mother and grandparents had tried to tell me. What a wedding day! However, sometime during the night, his mother and father told us to come in out of the cold. We lived there for the next several months.

Chapter 17

IT WAS NOT LONG AT ALL BEFORE the arguing and domestic violence started. We went to a club one night, and he kept disappearing. So when one of the guys there asked me to dance, I did. Of course, he would reappear when I was on the dance floor. He demanded that I cut the dance short, and he was ready to leave immediately. When we got in the car, he proceeded to hit me "for disrespecting him."

I discovered that night that he was very possessive. However, it was not at all unusual for me to see him flirting with some of the girls between classes in the hallways at school. I quickly learned that I had made the worst mistake that I ever had during my short lifetime.

His mother and father pastored a church, and we would go to church on Sundays. We would also go with them sometimes when they would fellowship with other churches, but our hearts and minds were not there.

I really was not feeling the church anymore after his father made a play on me one day when just he and I were in the house. I told my husband about it. He told me that his father had also tried to make a play on his older brother's wife.

On another occasion, I was awakened out of my sleep by his brother who had crept into our room and was trying to put his hands into my panties. I woke up and screamed, and he ran from the room.

It caused a disturbance, as my husband was awakened by my scream, and I explained to him what had happened. However, his brother denied it, and nothing more came of it.

Though we tried to go through the motions of what we thought a married couple should do, the fussing and fighting continued, and we both knew that the marriage was hopeless. He started going out and staying out until the wee hours of the morning sometimes, and when he came home, he was not in the mood for any lovemaking. I pretty much knew that there must be someone else he was seeing.

My husband did not mention anything about his father trying to seduce me, until one day when his mother and father were trying to intervene in one of our disagreements. His father was trying to chastise him for being gone so much; suddenly, he just blurted it out. It was a very uncomfortable moment with us all standing there. His mother did not say anything, and I really did not notice her treating me any differently, but I felt that she must have wanted me out of the house after that.

My husband had pretty much abandoned me at his parent's home by this time. He was only supposed to be working part-time after school not far from where we lived. But he came home later and later, and more and more tired. He rarely went to school anymore.

Chapter 18

WE MADE IT THROUGH THE WINTER, AND spring sprang, and so did spring fever.

I celebrated my seventeenth birthday on March 4 with my family, and later that month, I found out that my husband indeed had a mistress.

Our high school was located right before entering our one traffic light downtown area. The high-schoolers would walk downtown to buy lunch or hang out at the 7-Eleven convenience store during our lunchtime.

One day, I walked downtown with a couple of friends and saw my husband sitting in the window of one of the downtown apartment buildings with his shirt off. I was quickly informed that it was his mistress's apartment. It later seemed that everybody knew about the affair, except me.

His mistress was a twenty-five-year-old single mother with at least three children, who were said to all have different fathers. She had a reputation of sleeping with a variety of men, and even that she had gone to the city for a while and prostituted, before returning to West Virginia. To top it off, she had been the girlfriend of one of my husband's best friends, and his friend was very hurt by the betrayal.

This information somehow made me feel a little better. I felt that it made him look bad.

Although my mother and grandparents had told me that our marriage would not last, they made it known that if things did not work out, I could always come back home. I hated to admit that everyone was right, but I swallowed my pride and went back home brokenhearted and embarrassed.

The shame would only increase as my husband was frequently seen sitting in the window of his mistress's apartment during our lunch break or riding up and down the road with her. He totally quit going to school after our separation.

I was the talk of the school. I would oftentimes see people whispering, pointing, and snickering.

We were only together for five short months before we separated. But it was still very difficult for me to adjust to being back home, after being married. I was expected to resume where I had left off caring for my younger brothers and sister. I was also expected to start going back to church on Sundays and Wednesdays.

I was not only brokenhearted and ashamed, but I was also angry and bitter. Although I would do some things as before, I made up in my mind that things were not going to be the same. After all, I was an adult now, right?

Chapter 19

I CONTINUED TO GO TO SCHOOL. BUT EVERY weekend, I would hang out partying, getting high, and being promiscuous. It was not long before the school year ended, and I really started wilding out then. I convinced myself that I did not care about myself or what I did, but it was a lie from the pit of hell. That lie only helped me to dig a pit even deeper than the one I had been in most of my life.

I started skipping classes, and my grades dropped. But I was determined to graduate. I finished out my junior year and returned for my senior year. Our divorce was also finalized during my senior year, within a year of us getting married.

My mother wanted me to go to college right away, but I was not interested in school anymore. I enlisted and swore into the army during my senior year instead. I think I would have gone, if I could have gone right after graduation, but they had me wait until that fall before having me to report for my tour of duty. After all, I did not have a passion for serving in the military; I had just chosen it to avoid going to college. I had the whole summer to dread making this decision.

I had started seeing a guy who was eight years my elder during the summer after my separation. We were not faithful to each other, but he told me he loved me and did not want me to go away. He did not have any real goals in life and was living at home with his mother. But what he said made me not want to go that much more.

About a month or so before I was scheduled to go away, my mother's boyfriend had her to solicit me on his behalf. She told me that he said, "If I acted right, he would give me everything that I needed to go to the military." She told me that he was planning to come home with her after her 3:00 p.m.–11:00 p.m. shift that night, and he would talk to me more about it.

I knew exactly what she meant by "if I acted right," and I did not respond. I could not understand why she would allow herself to be used by him in that way. She had never done anything like this before. This made me feel worse than I already felt.

I had no intention of being home when they arrived that night. I felt that I had to confide in someone, so I told my boyfriend about the conversation. He and I had spent that evening together at our home and had fallen asleep on the couch. Before we knew what was happening, my mother and her boyfriend were coming into the house. We immediately got up and left. My mother and I never discussed what happened, and I was not propositioned again.

Chapter 20

THE TIME GOT CLOSER FOR ME TO go to the army, but I was determined to find a way to avoid it.

I called my recruiter and told him I was pregnant. He advised me that I would have to come in to take a pregnancy test. I went in to take the pregnancy test, but it was not my urine. I had a girlfriend who was pregnant, and I decided to ask her for a urine specimen so I could fake a pregnancy test. This was during a time when they did not check the temperature of urine or have someone watch or keep the restroom door open. Of course, I tested positive. I was off the hook, or so I thought.

Sometime later, my mother began to ask about my departure date to the army, and I confessed to her what I had done. She proceeded to contact my recruiter and told him about the deception. I did not know that she had contacted him, until he contacted me and let me know that he was aware of what I had done.

I called my mother on her job, crying and threatening to commit suicide. She politely told me to do what I felt I needed to do. I was not serious, so I did not attempt to take my life.

After the disclosure, my recruiter attempted to catch me at home at different times, to make me fulfill my obligation to serve in the army. I had sworn in after all.

Once he came to my grandparent's home when I was there. I am sure my mother had given him their address. My grandmother told him I was not there. She was not really a fan of me going in the army anyway.

After a while, the recruiter stopped trying to locate me. I have often wondered how my life would have turned out if I had gone into the army.

Chapter 21

ONE SUNDAY AFTER CHURCH, I RODE WITH my mother and other siblings to take my older brother back to college. Times like this were rare, since I had all but estranged myself from my family as I was trying to find my meaning and purpose in life. We had a very nice day together.

That evening after we had gotten back home, I hooked up with my boyfriend. The evening started off as usual, with us talking and getting high. He decided to drive up to the baseball field, like we sometimes did. But this time would be different.

I do not know what went through his mind, but suddenly he looked at me with the evilest look on his face that I had ever seen. It was as if a demon had possessed him. He started threatening me, and then he began to hit me. I am sure the enemy was planning to use him to kill me that day.

I tried asking him why he was doing this, but he just kept on hitting me. I tried to defend myself, but I was no match against this man who was almost a foot taller than I was and at least fifty pounds heavier.

I got out of the car and tried to run, but I still had the dress and heels on that I had worn to church earlier that day. It was easy for him to catch up to me.

One of my shoes came off, and he picked it up and began to hit me with the heel. He was hitting me on my back, my head, or wherever it landed. I was using my hands and arms to try and protect my head and face.

Suddenly, I felt a blow to my nose area, and I saw stars and blackness. I thought surely I was going to die that night. We were all alone on this field.

I cried out to God for help, and as suddenly as he started, he stopped hitting me. It was as if he blacked out and then came back to his senses. He told me he was going to take me home.

I was afraid to get back in the car with him but did not feel like I had a choice. It would have probably taken me over an hour to walk home. I was exhausted, and it was pitch-black dark along the road that I would have had to walk. There were not many streetlights up in the hollow where we lived.

He calmly drove me to my grandparents' home and dropped me off, not far from where he lived.

My grandmother got up and let me in the house, but the lights were out, and she was not able to see how bruised and disheveled I was. My body was aching all over, I felt like my head was spitting open. I went through to the room where we slept and into the bathroom to look at myself.

My face had already started to swell and was becoming discolored where the heel of my shoe had struck me beside my nose. I went to bed wondering how I was going to explain to my family what had happened to me. I did not get much sleep that night.

My grandfather had already left for work. But I got up before my grandmother the next morning, which was no easy task. I went into the bathroom to look at my face again, and it looked even worse than the night before. My nose looked like it was broken, my facial features were distorted on one side of my face, and my eye was black and almost swollen shut.

Anger began to well up inside of me. I felt like the demon that had possessed him the night before had come to possess me. It was as if I was having an out of body experience.

I got dressed and left the house quietly. I found a container with gas in it that was used to cut the grass. I poured some of the gas in a cup, and I took a box of matches with me. I was thinking, *He is not going to get away with what he's done to me. He is not going to ride up and down the road and do whatever he wants to do, as if he has done nothing.*

The dawning of day had just begun. I walked down the road, hoping that no one saw me. It was not that far to walk to my boyfriend's home, but I could not seem to walk fast enough. He parked his car across the road from their house, beside an old vacant house. I opened the driver's door of the car and poured the gasoline on the seat. I struck a match and threw it on the seat. The flame broke forth with a whoosh!

By this time, the day had gotten brighter. I could have easily been spotted by anyone who had awakened. I ran up the road a short distance to where a small bridge had been built connecting the road to the railroad tracks. I crossed over the bridge and continued to run up the railroad tracks, to get back to my grandparents' home before anyone saw me.

I frantically ran away from the scene of the crime and never looked back until I got back to my grandparents' house. As soon as I got in the yard, I looked back. I could see a huge black billow of smoke coming up from where I had set the car on fire. A few moments later, I began to hear the sirens of the fire trucks.

It was now time to face the music. My grandmother met me at the door. She saw my face, and she heard the sirens of the fire trucks. I explained how the two were connected and what had happened the night before. She was flabbergasted, and so was I and the rest of my family. It was all so very painful and embarrassing.

The swelling in my face went away in about a week, but it took over a month for the discoloration of my black eye to totally go away. I stayed in as much as possible, not wanting anyone to see my face.

I would love to say that I never had anything more to do with my boyfriend after this, but that would not be the truth. He started to call after a period. I would not talk to him for a while, but I eventually gave in and started to see him again. Of course, I was nervous about seeing him after all that had happened. But blind, battered, and broken, I went back to him.

Mental illness had a great effect on his family. There were five siblings. Two of his older brothers had seemed to be normal all through school, but sometime after graduating, they had schizophrenic break and were labeled as being "crazy" thereafter. His oldest brother suffered more in silence, but eventually committed suicide.

My boyfriend was able to hide it for the most part, but he struggled with mental illness as well. He never addressed it, but I knew that it was there. There was one winter season where he seemed to hear voices or to respond to some outside stimuli at certain times.

A couple of our mutual acquaintances had made comments concerning his mental instability during this time. Although they never came out and said what he had said or done. To this day, I do not know if he was taking medications for mental illness or not.

We continued to engage in our dysfunctional relationship until I left home. But we also knew that we were seeing other people.

Chapter 22

ONE DAY WHEN I WAS WALKING, I stopped to talk to a lady who had married into the family of some of my previous schoolmates. She told me that she was planning to go to cosmetology school and wanted somebody to ride with her. The school was almost an hour away.

I had never really thought about becoming a cosmetologist, but why not—I was not doing anything productive with my life at this point. So I agreed to go with her. I also liked to style hair.

The course would last a little over a year. We started the beginning of the year after I graduated from high school. I was able to receive financial aid and get a loan to pay for the schooling.

Cosmetology school occupied part of my time Tuesday through Saturday, but I still found time to continue to wild out and party.

One day when I was visiting a previous classmate, her nephew was at their home. He lived in Ohio but would come down periodically to visit his grandparents and other family members. He was my classmate's nephew, but he was older than we were. He ended up asking for my number when I was visiting one day, but I gave him the wrong number.

I really did not want any more drama in my life than what I already had. I had not personally met him before, but I knew that a girl in a grade ahead of me had had a son by him while we were still in school. I also knew that they were known to fight each other when they were out at clubs or other places when they saw one another with someone else.

I would see him from time to time at his grandparents' home or at the club after that initial meeting. He would always come up to me smiling and ask for my number again. I eventually gave in and gave him the right number, after he assured me that he and his "baby's mama" were no longer seeing each other.

He would look me up whenever he came into town. We would fool around until he went back home.

Over time, his trips became more frequent, and he would stay longer. He would ask me about going back with him, but I always told him no.

I graduated from cosmetology school in the summer of 1983. I found a job a short time later at The Hairstylist, in a mall about an hour away. I was not able to find a job any closer to home.

There was no public transportation, and I did not have a car, so I had to borrow my mother's car to get to work. My mother also had to use her car to get to work. Our schedules clashed oftentimes, as my work hours fluctuated. Sometimes I was extremely late, and there were times when I could not get there at all. I was not making much money and soon had to quit. I only worked there for about three months.

Chapter 23

F ALL WAS BEGINNING TO EMERGE, AND I did not know what I was
going to do with myself. I could possibly find another job, but I
would end up facing the same challenges that I had faced at my previous job. The lady whom I went to cosmetology school with would
eventually end up with her own shop, but that would not be until
after I left home. She failed her initial state board exam and had to
schedule to take it over.

I went to church one night and rededicated my life to the Lord.
I even started to sing in our little family choir that my grandmother
had started.

It was during this time that I was approached by my family
molester for the first time. I finally found the courage to stand up
to him. I made it clear that what had been happening over the years
was wrong and never should have happened. I also made it clear that
it would never happen again, and it never did. He did not like it,
but I did not care. I was finally proclaiming my freedom from this
incestual bondage.

I had been converted, but I was not filled with the Holy Ghost,
and it was not long before I slid back into my old lifestyle of drinking, drugging, and partying. But I knew that I wanted more in life
than this. I had to somehow break this vicious cycle and develop into

the woman whom I was created to be. I knew God had a plan for me. But of course, the plan would not unfold overnight.

My previous classmate's nephew made a trip to West Virginia right after Thanksgiving that year and asked me to go back with him to Ohio again. I said yes that time. It seemed to be the only way for me to get out of the rut I was in and get a fresh start.

The night before we left for Ohio, I asked him to take me to my grandparents' home so I could tell them that I was leaving. My mother was out of town attending training, so she would have to find out later. My grandfather told me that he did not think it was a good idea and warned me against going. But I had my mind made up.

Chapter 24

I WAS BACK IN OHIO, BUT INSTEAD OF Cleveland, I was in Columbus this time. It was soon after Thanksgiving, and the weather was getting cold. I was a little anxious about how things would turn out, but I was also excited about the new possibilities. I had missed the city—the public transportation, the bright lights, and paved roads and sidewalks everywhere.

We moved in with his mother and two of his younger brothers. Right away, I started looking for a job. I knew I could not live anywhere for free, not for long anyway. We applied for public assistance until we could find jobs.

I was hoping to get a job as a cosmetologist, but someone at the Ohio state cosmetology licensing board told me that I would have to take their state board exam before I could get a license there. I did not have the time, money, or courage to sit for another state board so soon. I later found out that the person who told me that was wrong. The West Virginia state board required 1,800 hours for a licensed cosmetologist, whereas Ohio only required 1,500. I could have been granted reciprocity and issued a license without having to take their state board exam.

I would learn that everything happens for a reason. Even though I liked styling hair, my vocational calling was not to be a cosmetologist.

My mother and oldest brother drove up a few months after I moved to Columbus. I found out that my father had been sent to the prison there after shooting a woman he had gotten into an altercation with. He did not kill her but had apparently shot her in the rear end. We went to see him while they were there. They only stayed a few days before returning to West Virginia.

It took some time, but I got a job at the Sheraton Hotel downtown as a steward in the dish room (the cage) on Valentine's Day of the following year. The same day that I applied for the job, I was put to work. I was expecting to apply for some jobs and then go back home to enjoy some Valentine's Day candy, but the job was more important.

I wish I could say that things went smoothly after I moved to Columbus, but that would not be the truth. It was not long before domestic violence started. Quite often it was because he had gotten drunk and wanted to fight for whatever reason he came up with.

I hated violence and loved my peace, but I was not one to let someone beat me to a bloody pulp—I fought back. Sometimes when his mother or brothers were home, they would try to intervene. But this would usually make matters worse.

I seemed to attract abusive men, which makes me believe, as I heard later, women oftentimes end up with men who are like their fathers. He was also a heavy drinker and a cheater.

He was not the only one violent in his family; it seemed that most of his family members were short-fused as well. It was not unusual for any of them to end up fighting with each other.

Chapter 25

I BECAME ACQUAINTED WITH MY FEMALE SUPERVISOR AT the Sheraton, who was a few years older than I was. One day, I came to work with a black eye, and she immediately had empathy for me. She had been in an abusive relationship herself. She encouraged me to get away from him. I was not making enough money to get a place of my own, so I stayed. I guess I could have gone back to West Virginia, but I vowed never to go back home to stay.

The fighting did not get any better, and one day, my supervisor invited me to come and live with her and her sister and their three children. I was not thrilled about the idea, but I knew that I needed to get away. But I did not know how I would ever be able to pack my things and get away without anyone being home; after all, I did not have a car, and neither did my supervisor.

One night, my boyfriend and his mother got into an altercation, and she called the police, and they arrested him. That was my chance to get away. I packed my things as quickly as I could and called a coworker to come and pick me up. I had finally gotten away, at least for now.

I moved in with my supervisor and her family and contributed to the household the best I could. I had worked at the Sheraton Hotel for several months when I realized that it was time for a change. I knew this was not the type of work I wanted to do the rest of my life. I was working part-time hours and barely making more than minimum wage. I wanted to get my own place, but I would never be able to do so at this rate.

I started thinking about going to college, to become the nurse that I had dreamed to be since I was five years old. I also knew that becoming a nurse would provide me with a stable income. I applied for financial aid and enrolled to start college in the fall of 1984.

My previous boyfriend found out where I was living during the summer. One day, he rode by and saw me sitting on the porch. He tried off and on all summer to get me to come back to him, but I did not want to go back to live in that volatile situation. But foolishly, I went out with him a few times throughout the summer. I also dated a couple of other guys during the summer. Shaking my head!

I started college as planned that fall. I worked at the Sheraton during the day and went to college at night. I was still living with my supervisor and her two boys. Her sister had moved out.

After a while, her boyfriend got out of jail and moved back in. Things seemed to be peaceful for a while. But I came home one night, and no one was home. I could sense that something was wrong, but I did not know what.

I found out the next morning that my supervisor's boyfriend had started being abusive to her again. She let me know that she was hiding from him and would not be able to keep renting the home that we lived in.

I was between a rock and a hard place. I did not have anywhere else to go. I could not afford my own place. Someone told me about the YMCA, but even that would have been too expensive for me at that time. I was not working for many hours.

I was trying to figure out what I was going to do when my previous boyfriend showed up one day. He asked me to come back to him and promised that things would be different. I really did not believe him, but I did not have many options. My mother was right: "Once abusive, always abusive." At least it was true in our relationship.

I felt uncomfortable going back to his mother's house to live, especially after the way I had left. But I talked to his mother about coming back, and she said I could. I let her know that I would contribute to the household as much as possible.

Chapter 26

M Y BOYFRIEND AND I PLANNED TO GET our own place as soon as we could, even though I was not feeling it. I was with him out of necessity. I was playing a role. He worked different jobs off and on. He was always quitting jobs or getting fired. I continued to work and go to college.

I suddenly started feeling nauseated and drained, and it lasted all day and then every day. What I feared was true—I was pregnant. I had always wanted children, but this was not the right time or situation. But what did I expect? After all, I was playing the role. I did not believe in abortions, so I would just have to deal with it.

My boyfriend was okay with the pregnancy, but he made it clear that he was not sure the baby was his. Even though we had gotten together a few times after we separated, we had not been back together for very long. We knew that we both had dated other people while we were separated, but I was the one pregnant. We had many heated discussions about this throughout my pregnancy. I hoped the baby was his.

I started spotting during my first trimester and was told by my doctor that I was doing too much. I was advised to either quit working or attending school. I was just finishing the first semester in college. So I decided to keep working and postpone school until after my pregnancy. It would take me longer than expected, but I was determined to finish college. I would prove to my mother and myself that I was not a quitter.

Regardless of how he felt, my boyfriend went with me to all my prenatal appointments, and he was even there all night during the delivery of our son. He would be there for all three of our children's births.

I was able to see our son's undeniable resemblance to his father as soon as he was born, and so was his father. Everyone who saw our baby boy commented about how much he looked like his dad, and he still does today, although I've always thought he had my eyes. I vowed never to get myself in a serious questionable situation like this again, and I did not.

I wish I could say that everything went smoothly during the labor and delivery, but that's not how it went. My water had started a slow leak the morning before my son was born, but being my first child, I didn't know that it was something to be concerned about. I did not start to have contractions until that night, and my doctor told me to come in for the delivery.

My labor lasted all night, and our son was born at 9:04 a.m. the next morning. He seemed to be doing fine, but the day that I was scheduled to go home, the staff realized that my son was running a fever and could not be sent home. They found out that my son had contracted a strep infection during the time that my water was leaking.

He had to stay in the hospital for two weeks after he was born to be treated with a course of intravenous antibiotics. They ended up shaving both sides of his head to access the various needle sites they would have to use over the two-week treatment course. They explained that baby's scalp veins are bigger than the veins in their hands and feet, and babies move their arms and legs so much that it is hard to keep a catheter in place in those areas. I felt so bad for him. I went to see him as often as I could. The hospital was quite a distance from where we lived, and I did not have a car at the time. I had to wait until his father got home from work or wherever he was and felt like going to see him.

Finally, it was time for him to come home. They were sure that the infection was all cleared up and he was no longer running a fever. I was able to start bonding with my son. He was home for two weeks, and then he started to run a fever again. We took him to the hospital, and after running some tests, they found that the infection had come back with a vengeance. He had to be hospitalized for two more weeks, and the hair that had just started to grow back had to be shaved off again.

I thank God that he was healthy throughout his childhood. I never had to take him to the emergency department again while he was growing up for any sicknesses or injuries.

Chapter 27

MY SON WAS BORN IN JUNE OF 1985. I started back to college that fall. I quit my job at the Sheraton Hotel and enrolled in the work-study program at the college I was attending.

During the time I was attending college, domestic violence continued. There were times when I went to school with bruises and scratches, but I was determined to keep going.

My boyfriend had gotten a decent-paying job working for the city, and we had gotten our own apartment while I was in school.

Several months before I was scheduled to graduate, my boyfriend had become surprisingly nicer. He rarely raised his voice and was hardly ever violent. I had started to feel less threatened by him and had become fond of him. The change seemed genuine, but he had made the comment that someone told him that after I graduated and got a job, I was going to leave him. Although I had never told anyone, I had that thought on more than a few occasions.

I ran into some babysitting issues now and then and had to miss another quarter along the way, but I managed to graduate and get my registered nursing degree in June of 1988.

My father came from Cleveland, and my mother came from West Virginia to attend my nursing graduation. My mother brought my niece with her. My sister had her during her senior year in high school. My mother and grandmother had agreed to keep her while she went off to college. She was two years old like my son. My parents lodged with us during their stay. However, they still could not agree on anything. But it was good to see them, and I truly felt honored that they had taken the time to come. They both gave me fifty dollars as a graduation gift.

I had been offered a job by the director of nursing at the hospital I did my clinicals at during my last quarter in school. She said she liked my professionalism and the way I cared for my patients. After I graduated and took my state board exam, I applied for a position on her unit and was hired. At that time, it took approximately six weeks to get the results of our exams back. But we could be hired on our temporary student nurse credentials in the meantime. I was scheduled to start my new job two to three weeks after I graduated.

I was still smoking marijuana and drinking alcohol almost daily while I was attending nursing school. I had even experimented with crack cocaine. It became popular on the streets in the 1980s and was more readily available than marijuana at times. My boyfriend introduced it to me laced in a cigarette. I experimented with it several times, but I did not like the high. It made me feel too jittery. I learned that it was very addictive. But I thank God that I did not get hooked on it like so many family members and friends did. I realize that it was nothing but the grace of God.

During the time between graduating and starting my new job, the Lord started dealing with me very strongly. I could feel an overwhelming urge to dedicate my life to Him. I felt that He was telling me I needed to start fresh with my new career and a new life. The drugs and alcohol did not seem to get me high anymore. They just seemed to make me paranoid and feel convicted. I was getting ready to start a career where I would be encouraging others to steer clear of substance abuse, but I was using substances myself.

One night while I was getting high with my boyfriend, I felt my spirit leave my body, and I was able to look down at myself sitting on the couch. The experience really frightened me—it seemed as if the Lord was telling me to give my life to Him, or else. I did not know the specifics of what "or else" was, but I did not want to find out. I made it up in my mind that I was going to church the next Sunday.

Chapter 28

I WENT TO CHURCH THE NEXT SUNDAY AS planned. I do not remember what the message was about, but as soon as the altar call was made, I found myself heading toward the front of the church. I repented of my sins and rededicated my life to the Lord. I needed a fresh start that only the Lord could give. When I started my job a week or so later, for the most part, I felt clean with a clear conscience. I quit drinking and drugging cold turkey. I had been washed in the blood of Jesus!

Although I felt guilt-free in one area of my life, I knew that fornication and "shacking up" was wrong. I knew that I could not continue to live the way I had been living.

I told my boyfriend that I had gotten saved, and we could not continue to have sex without being married. He had no problem with getting married. He had mentioned it a couple of times before. But I was not so sure that we should. Yes, he was my son's father, but I did not think I loved him the way that I should. Also, the violence had decreased, but I was not so sure that it would not start up again.

I fleeced the Lord like Gideon. I prayed and asked the Lord if I should marry him. I also prayed that the Lord would give me a sign. Later that same day, I was looking at a Christian program on television, and the message was about not being unequally yoked with an unbeliever. I felt in my spirit that this was my answer from the Lord. I cannot say that my boyfriend did not believe in God, because he would occasionally go to church, but that was the extent of it.

I saw red flags signaling to me that I should not plunge into marriage right away, but I leaned to my own understanding and did not allow the Lord to direct my path. I felt that I could grow to love him more, and after all, he was my son's father.

We were married by a justice of the peace two months after I rededicated my life to the Lord.

I do not know how it would have turned out if I had followed the guidance of the fleece and the red flags, but it was only a short time before I realized that I had made a drastic mistake! One that I would feel the repercussions from for years to come.

We had a reception at his mother's home a couple of weeks after we were married and invited family and friends to come and help us celebrate our union. We took a lot of pictures during the event, and I was excited about displaying the pictures in our home. However, at the end of the celebration when mostly everyone had gone home, we realized that the camera was missing. Someone had apparently stolen it. I was devastated! It seemed like a bad omen.

Chapter 29

S OON AFTER WE WERE MARRIED, MY HUSBAND started staying out later and later after work, until some nights he did not come home at all. I discovered that the other woman was a derivative of cocaine, the "white lady"—crack. I also discovered that not only had he become addicted to it but also his brothers, brother-in-law, mother, and her husband.

I had heard of the devastating effects this drug could have on people. My husband had previously told me about how one of his coworkers had lost his nice home, wife, and kids because of his addiction. He had also told me about his friend's girlfriend whose career was destroyed due to her addiction. I had not experienced the effects of it firsthand, but I would.

I went to bed one night exhausted after working a three to eleven shift at the hospital and awakened the next morning, realizing that I had been robbed. My purse had been removed from the bedside where I always put it before going to bed. I went through the house looking for it in case I had inadvertently left it somewhere else, but it was nowhere to be found. My husband seemed to be just as surprised about it as I was. He swore no one else had been in the house that night, and the doors were locked. He pointed out that the screen on the window on the back door looked as if it had been cut.

Nothing else in the house seemed to be missing or tampered with. We filed a police report, but nothing came of it.

When I told my mother about it, she told me that she thought it was an inside job. I never knew what happened, but I kept my mother's thoughts in mind. It was really frightening to think of someone coming into our home and upstairs into our bedroom to steal my purse. They would have had to come right next to the bed where I kept my purse while I was sleeping! We had only recently moved into the town house, and it took me a long while for me to really feel comfortable there. I felt violated.

My husband became more and more addicted, and he also continued to drink heavily. It started to be a habit for him to miss work the day after he got paid. He even started to miss days in between. I would usually find out about it when he would blurt it out during some conversation we were having. For some reason, he was convinced that the city could not fire him, and he would tell me so. Eventually, the inevitable happened, and he lost his job. He tried to persuade me that he was wrongfully fired, and he should fight it in court. He said they fired him because he was not wearing goggles in a dangerous area where they had been mandated to wear them. He said he was not wearing his goggles because someone had taken them. Oh, how naive I was. We had not been married long, and I wanted to prove to him that I was a good wife, so I hired a lawyer to fight to get his job back.

Around two thousand dollars later in lawyer fees, I found out in court that the reason they terminated my husband was totally different from what he had told me. His employer pulled out a file about as thick as an encyclopedia with all the infractions he had accumulated during his employ. They explained how they had tried over and over to work with him to no avail. They finally disclosed how he had been seen on camera breaking into other employees' lockers and taking items out of them. What a waste of time and money. He never stood a chance of getting his job back.

The loss of income impacted our home. But he had started giving less toward the household expenses before he was fired. He would make up excuses as to why he could not give as much as he agreed.

Now all the household expenses were on me. He would get jobs here and there, but nothing as good as his job with the city. He could not really hold down a job anymore due to his addiction. Thank God, I was still able to make ends meet during the many times he was unemployed or just not contributing to the household.

Chapter 30

THE EAST COAST HAD A TERRIBLE ICE storm that struck on the eve of February 7, 1989; it impacted Ohio as well as West Virginia. I called my grandmother before I got ready to go to bed that evening and asked if my mother was still there. My grandmother told me she had just left to go home. She asked if I wanted her to go next door and get her, but I told her not to bother going out into the bad weather. I let her know that I did not have anything pressing I needed to talk to her about. This was one of the times my mother did not have phone service.

My grandmother kept my niece while my mother worked at the hospital. My mother would go to my grandmother's house to pick her up when she got off from work. Sometimes, she would stay and talk for a while before going home next door.

The storm lasted all night. I knew because I got very little sleep that night. I kept dozing off and waking up. When I would awaken, it seemed as if my spirit was grieving. I felt compelled to pray several times during the night, but I did not really know what to pray for. My husband had not gotten home, but I had grown accustomed to him staying out most of the night or even all night over the past months. Usually, if I called his mother's home, he would be there. There was something else I was grieving about, but what could it be?

I felt mentally and spiritually exhausted when I got up for work the next morning. My husband had gotten a ride home while I was getting ready for work. This was one of the times he was not working. He stayed home with our son when I left for work. I would have had to take our son to my sister-in-law if he had not made it home in time. I did not realize just how bad it was outside, but on my way to work, I had to detour off my usual route, because they had blocked off some of the roads due to extremely slippery conditions.

I got to work safely, but I felt drained. I still felt like I was grieving over something terrible that had happened. I talked to my Christian coworker about what I had experienced that night and was still experiencing that morning. I made it to lunchtime, and my coworker and I went down to the cafeteria together. When we were getting on the elevator to go back to our work unit, we suddenly saw our director of nursing and my husband getting on the elevator we were on. I started to ask what was going on but was told to wait until we got back to our floor. I was about to find out what I had been grieving about.

I was informed that my mother had been killed in a car accident on her way to work that morning due to the ice storm. Her car had slid across the icy road and flipped over into the half-frozen creek. We were later told that she had probably been knocked unconscious with the impact and drowned. My youngest brother who was in the car with her almost lost his life as well. But he was thrown out of the car when it crashed and was found floating on the water when the paramedics arrived. Thank God the paramedics were able to revive him, or we would have suffered two deaths.

The loss of our mother was surreal. I was too young to lose my mother; I was only twenty-five years old. Our relationship had just started to grow closer. It had not been long since she had started communicating with me as an adult and not with the daughter whom she felt compelled to criticize whenever possible, or that's how I viewed it anyway. We had gotten, so we could talk and laugh with each other, as women and friends. I would have an unfulfilled void the rest of my life, missing the mother I had come to know as my friend.

When my older brother and I arrived in West Virginia, we were called on to coordinate the arrangements for our mother's memorial service and burial. He had been living in Texas. We did not have a clue of what to do, but we had a few people to offer guidance through the process. Our grandmother was very helpful, even though I knew she was grieving the loss of her oldest daughter as well. She said she was dreaming about the accident when she was awakened by the ringing of the phone and informed that the accident she was dreaming about had really occurred. My grandmother was a dreamer, and she could also interpret her dreams.

My faith through the grace of God helped me to deal with the loss of our mother.

Chapter 31

Within a year, I experienced several events the professionals identify as major life stressors. I had started a new career, got married, and lost my mother within a year, but it was not over yet. I would soon discover that I had gotten pregnant the month after my mother died.

When I was about four months pregnant, my husband agreed to get some help with his crack addiction that was continually getting worse. I arranged through my medical insurance for him to go to a drug rehabilitation center in Texas called Rapha. He was supposed to be there for a month. I was so hopeful that he would be able to kick the habit, and we could find some type of normalcy in our marriage. But the day that he was scheduled to catch his flight to Texas, he informed me that he had decided not to go.

He convinced me that he had not really tried to quit up to this point and promised that he would kick the habit on his own. But it was just another promise that he would break. He seemed to be doing so well for a while, but soon it seemed as if the addiction was worse than ever. We were on a roller-coaster ride that would not end. Even when he tried to withstand the urges, his family members would call and lure him out of our home, and it would start all over again.

I was still attending church, praying, and reading my Bible on a regular basis, and that is where I found the peace and strength to endure the trials and tests that were ever present in my life.

My grandmother in West Virginia had referred me to the church. The pastor was the daughter of a woman of God whom my grandmother used to listen to every Sunday morning on a local television station. Her husband was the prophet of the church.

He prophesied that I would have "the baby girl that I had always wanted." It was true. I had always wanted a girl that I could dress pretty and put ribbons in her hair.

He also prophesied to me that the Lord was going to heal the condition in my body. The condition was asthma. I had "outgrown" it when I was about nine years old, but it recurred after I started smoking cigarettes and marijuana.

The doctors had to keep increasing my medication dosages, but the symptoms seemed to grow worse. Even after I stopped smoking, the symptoms did not get any better. The doctor told me he could not increase the dosages anymore because it could cause serious adverse reactions. I could not leave home without my inhaler. It was my security blanket, and I had to take pills every day.

After I was prophesied to, I had faith in what the prophet told me. I went home and threw my inhaler and pills in the trash. However, before the day was over, I had another asthma attack and had to get my medication out of the trash. Even though the healing was not manifested that day, I kept believing in my healing.

A short time later, we were heading out of town. The trip was spur of the moment, and I had to pack in a hurry. We had gotten far away from home when I realized I had forgotten my inhaler. I started to panic, but I heard a still small voice that told me everything was going to be alright, and it was! I have never had another asthma attack. God is a healer!

Chapter 32

MY COWORKERS THREW AN AWESOME BABY SHOWER for me and two other nurses who were expecting on our unit. Although there were three of us, I got more than enough for our soon to arrive baby girl, including a baby bed.

I gave birth to our oldest daughter the same year my mother died on December 7, 1989. Oh, how I wished they could have met. I had the daughter I had always dreamed of. I always wanted a daughter I could dress pretty and put fancy hairbows in her hair.

The hospital arranged for my husband and I to have a candlelight dinner before our daughter and I were discharged from the hospital. That was something they did for the proud new parents. I informed him of the occasion, and he promised to be there. I waited all day, excited about the event that evening, but he never showed up; he was missing in action. The other woman had won again (crack cocaine). Of course, I was heartbroken and even embarrassed as the hospital staff came to escort us to the special occasion. I ended up eating the meal in my hospital room alone.

He showed up the next day to take us home. He was full of apologies and excuses for not showing up for dinner, but it left a wound that would not quickly heal. I felt so hopeless and helpless. I really did not know how much more I could take. But I decided to try to hold it together at least for a while longer; after all, we had just had our baby girl, and we had only been married about a year and a half.

I thought about having my tubes tied after the birth of our daughter. I really could not imagine having any more children with him. He was so irresponsible, and he would not even discuss being admitted to a treatment center again. However, I was only twenty-six years old, so I decided to try the diaphragm instead.

I went back to work before my six-week postpartum period was up. I did not have much of a choice. I had two children I had to provide for now. My husband was not a provider. He would work for a while and then quit or get fired. When he was working, his money was spent on crack. If he made it home on payday, he would give me some money for the bills and then come back later demanding it back.

He would also take things from the house sometimes to sell for crack. One of my coworkers had bought our daughter a nice outfit. She had left the receipt in the bag in case it was not the right size and I needed to exchange it. When I tried it on her, it just fit her, so I decided to exchange it for a larger size so she could get more wear out of it. I left the bag in the trunk so it would already be in there when I went to the store the next day. That night, he took the car while I was asleep. When he returned, the outfit was missing. I was really hurt that he would take our daughter's gift and sell it for crack.

On another occasion, he had taken a train set that I had bought our son for Christmas. When I realized it was missing, I guess I raised such a ruckus that he came back with a replacement that day.

I bought a nice used car with some of the insurance money from my mother's death. I gave my husband my old car, since his car had been repossessed not long after losing his job with the city. I was glad to have two cars again because sometimes I would have to wait extended periods of time before he would come and pick me up after work. Sometimes he would rent the car out for crack.

One night after getting off work, I saw the car that I gave my husband ahead of me on the road, and thinking my husband was driving it, I blew my horn to get his attention. I followed the car for quite a distance before finally getting them to stop.

Once they stopped, I realized that my husband was not even in the car. There were about three strange young guys in the car. I told the driver that he did not have any business driving the car and foolishly demanded the keys and threatened to call the police. He told me he was not going to give me the keys as they were far from their home, and they said they had rented the car from my husband. He told me that if I was willing to follow them back to their home, they would give me the keys. I was so upset, I foolishly followed them to their destination. Thankfully, he was not violent, and he gave me the keys like he promised. I later thought about how they could have hurt or killed me challenging them like I did.

Chapter 33

M y Christian friend whom I worked with was a source of strength for me. We would frequently talk about what I was going through, and she would always find the words to encourage me. I visited her church once or twice.

When she found a new job and left the hospital, I really missed her. But we kept in touch, and it was not long before she encouraged me to come and apply for a job at the nursing home where she had been hired as the director of nursing.

I worked at the hospital for two years and had worked out the terms of the bonus I received when I was employed. I was excited about getting a new job. Especially since I was increasingly scheduled more three to eleven shifts, instead of the seven to three shifts I was hired for. The three to eleven shift was difficult for me to work having young children. I did not get a chance to spend much time with them when I worked that shift.

I filled out an application at the nursing home and was immediately hired as the day shift supervisor. Of course, my friend had a lot to do with it. She told me she knew I was a hard worker, and I would be able to handle the position. I would now be working three twelve-hour shifts from 7:00 a.m. until 7:00 p.m., instead of the five eight-hour shifts that I was scheduled at the hospital. They were long shifts, but at least I would be off four days a week.

I would be supervising nurses that were many years my senior, mostly licensed practical nurses after only being a nurse for two years. Some of the nurses made sure I knew they were not pleased with me being their supervisor and made snide remarks at first, but they soon got to know me as being helpful and easy to get along with, and we worked well together.

Chapter 34

BY THE END OF THE SUMMER, I felt that I had taken all the stress and disappointment of my marriage that I could. Even though I was nervous about trying to raise our children alone, I thought it could not be any worse than what I was going through. The drug use was at an all-time high, and he still would not agree to getting any help. Nearly all the financial, physical, and emotional burdens of running a home were on me.

I also knew that he was running around with other women, and so did his family and friends. His mother called me one day and asked me why I did not speak to her the night before when she waved to me in our car. Of course, it was not me. He was sitting beside me on the bed when she asked me the question, and I backhanded him in the mouth before I even thought about what I was doing. He did not even attempt to retaliate. I later had to go to the emergency room because my hand was hurting so bad. I had to receive treatment for a "boxer's fracture."

On one of his paydays, he gave me some money for the bills and left. Later that night, he came back home demanding that I give him the money he had given me. When I did not give him the money right away, he grabbed my purse and took the money back and ran down the stairs to get in the car and leave again. I looked out of the bedroom window and saw a woman sitting in the car waiting for him.

I did something very foolish that night. I grabbed our two children and ran out of the house after him, barefooted, in my house dress. I threw the children in my car and engaged in a high-speed chase trying to catch up with him. He drove to his sister's house, and they jumped out of the car and ran inside. However, by the time I got myself and the children out of the car and followed them inside, they were nowhere to be found. I believe they ran out of the back door.

I waited a while for him to come back knowing that he would eventually have to come back for the car, but he did not come back while I was there. I know it was for the best. There is no telling what would have transpired if he had. And whatever would have happened would not have been worth it. He was not trying to change.

His sister was still my substitute babysitter. She would often talk to me and tell me that her brother did not deserve me, and she would fully understand if one day I decided to leave him. This was one of those times.

I finally decided to leave him. I looked for affordable apartments in the area and found one not too far from my job. I made time to go and look for new furniture because some of the furniture we had was what he purchased when he was working for the city a few years earlier, and I did not want to take anything with me that I had not paid for.

I strategically planned to move on a day when I was off, and he was scheduled to work. However, ironically the morning that I was scheduled to move, he decided to call out for work. I really had to do some quick restrategizing. I had to sneak and call the movers and cancel the move. I also called the furniture store and told them not to call the house. I asked them to meet me at the new apartment during a certain time.

I made an excuse for having to leave the house and was able to successfully meet the guys at the new apartment for the delivery.

However, when I got back home, my husband informed me that he had gotten a call concerning the furniture delivery despite me asking them not to call my home. There were no cell phones in 1990.

I confessed that I was fed up with the way things were and he was not trying to change, so I had decided to leave him.

He did not seem to be very upset. He told me I should have let him know that I was leaving so he could have had time to arrange for somewhere else to go. However, I knew it would not have been that simple if I had informed him of my plan.

We had a long talk about everything, and I told him that I did not plan to change my mind. However, I agreed to let him stay with us in our new apartment for thirty days until he could find a place of his own. This was not what I had planned, and of course, it did not work out that way.

Later that month, I started being nauseated all day, and my monthly did not come. I knew I was pregnant, but I did not even want to get tested. How could this happen? I would hardly let him touch me, and when I did, I would always use the diaphragm that I had received after my first daughter was born. But there were times when I would go to bed exhausted and later wake up to the realization that he was having sex with me or had had sex with me.

I did not want to have another child by him. I did not need another mouth to feed. I did not need another child to have to arrange babysitting for while I worked. I did not have a reliable babysitter for the two children I already had who were now five and eight months old.

I did not tell anyone about my pregnancy for a while, nor did I get a pregnancy test. I still did not believe in abortions, but I secretly wished that I would have a miscarriage.

Chapter 35

FINALLY, THE THIRTY DAYS WERE UP FOR my husband to find another place to live, but I knew he had not been saving his money. We discussed our agreement that morning as we both left for work, and I asked for the key he had to the apartment. I got off work and picked the children up from the babysitter. We had done our usual evening routine and gone to bed. I had not heard anything from him all day.

It had to be about one or two o'clock in the morning when I heard loud knocking at the door. When I went downstairs and looked through the peep hole, all I could see was a police officer.

I opened the door to see what was going on, and there was my husband standing next to him with his clothes torn and blood running down his face. He was also missing a couple of teeth.

I tried to tell the police officer that he no longer officially lived there, but somehow, I ended up letting him come in so the police officer could go on his way. I was still determined that we could not stay together and go on the way things had been; it had taken too much of a toll on me. Somehow, someway, I had to get away from him!

I let him know in no uncertain terms that him staying there longer was only temporary. But I was too exhausted to keep fighting about it at that time. I had to maintain enough strength to take care of everything else I had going on at the time.

I had not fully rested up from the recent move and had gone right back to work. My job had become more strenuous. I was now expected to work part of the skilled nursing unit in addition to performing my supervisor duties and was constantly on my feet. It was also exhausting having to get up extra early in the morning to get the children ready and take them to the babysitter and pick them up and take them home after a long day at work. Oh, and not to mention the pregnancy thing.

I had started to show a little, and I was still having morning sickness all day long. I finally went to get a pregnancy test. It was just for confirmation, but I also knew that I needed to start getting prenatal care.

I finally told my husband, my in-laws, and my family that I was pregnant. This time I was not as happy or hopeful about my pregnancy as the times before, but I would just have to get there. Abortion was not an option.

Chapter 36

OUR MARRIAGE DID NOT GET ANY BETTER during my pregnancy. My husband was still drinking, drugging, and womanizing. I tried to make myself feel better by promising myself that after the baby was born, I would get out of the marriage once and for all. But I have to admit I was somewhat anxious about having to manage the children all on my own.

I continued to go to church, read the Word, and pray on a regular basis, but I found it to be more and more difficult with all the distractions. The prophet at the church I was attending prophesied to me that God was going to remove what was distracting me, and he urged me to continue to seek a closer relationship with God.

About six months after I started to work at the nursing home, the state inspectors started coming around. They had gotten complaints from some of the residents about some issues they were displeased with. Sometimes they would show up early in the morning and stay until late in the evening looking for deficiencies.

Within a month or two, they had found enough deficiencies to close the place down. The residents had to be moved to other nursing homes, and the staff were without jobs.

I was seven months pregnant without a job. We did not even get a severance package. I had to do something quick, but who would hire someone who was seven months pregnant?

My husband had just recently quit a job because "he did not like the way he was being treated." However, just a week or so before, he was bragging about how the supervisor liked him and his work. That was a pattern with him. I learned that whenever he started talking good about a job, it would not be long before he would either quit or get fired.

I started to panic. Within a week, I had signed up for welfare, signed up for unemployment, and signed up with a nursing agency.

I knew welfare came with food stamps and a check, but it would not be enough to pay the rent, utilities, and all the other household expenses.

I was told by unemployment that they would only pay up until two weeks before I was due to deliver because I would not have been able to work after that time.

The nursing agency was what really came through for me. I knew I could make up to a certain amount of money while receiving unemployment, but they were calling me almost every day to works shifts for them. I turned them down for some of the shifts, but I knew I would not be able to work much longer before I would have my baby.

It was at a low-rated nursing home, and it was hard to get nurses to work there. The smell of urine and or feces would hit your nose as soon as you walked through the door. Also, the cooling system was not working properly, and the tube feedings would curdle in the tubing. Those are just a couple of things that made the nurses refuse to work there, but I was desperate.

I soon realized that I was making more money than unemployment allowed, but I needed to build a nest egg that would carry our household while I was on maternity leave. If there was music to be faced, I would have to face it later.

The workload was so hard there, I did not get a chance to eat lunch or sit down during the whole eight-hour shift. I had to make sure I ate before I got there. It felt like my pelvic bone was going to split right down the middle by the time my shift ended. At least my husband was helping with the babysitting, and sometimes he would have cooked and did some cleaning while I was at work.

Chapter 37

I worked up until it was time to deliver our baby. I worked on May twenty-third nineteen ninety-one and our baby was born on the twenty-fourth. The contractions started around ten or eleven o'clock that morning and it did not take long for them to become more frequent and more painful. I knew quite quickly that this labor would not take as long as the other two.

My husband was not home at the time, but I was able to get in contact with him and let him know that my labor had started. He would have to take me to the hospital and care for our other two children while I was in the hospital.

I hurried to finish braiding our daughter's hair, so no one would have to worry about fixing it while I was in the hospital. After I finished her hair, I got myself ready to go to the hospital. By that time the pain had gotten so intense that I started pacing the floor. Our little seventeen-month-old daughter was running alongside me crying for me to pick her up, but I was in too much pain.

It was not too long before my husband got home, and we had to leave right away.

He wanted to be there for the delivery, so we had to drop the children off at his mother's house on the way to the hospital. One thing I can say about him is that he was there for each one of our children's births. I think he was there for his oldest son's birth as well. I guess he was amazed by the miracle of childbirth, or maybe he was truly trying to be supportive.

After I got checked in, they took me straight to the birthing room. I had dilated to eight centimeters. An intern started asking me questions, and right in the middle of his assessment, my water broke with a loud *whoosh*. He jumped back and ran out of the room to get my doctor. Our daughter was born a short time later.

She was a beautiful little girl with a head full of silky black hair. I was glad I had another girl, because I still had a lot of clothes that her sister had quickly outgrown, and they were practically new. She was a good baby. She did not cry very much at all.

I decided to go with the Norplant birth control method this time. I did not want to have any more children, especially not with him.

I asked to be released a day early from the hospital so I could hurry home and get prepared for my older brother and his wife to come visit. They had driven from Texas. They stopped in West Virginia first to visit with our grandparents, and they were coming to visit us in Ohio next. They were expected to arrive just three days after our daughter was born.

I started cleaning and preparing the area where my brother and his wife would sleep the day after I got home with the baby. My husband helped some, but then he decided he had somewhere to go. I told him I would need to go to the store to pick up some last-minute items after he got back.

We were down to one car again, but I thought for sure he would come back in a decent amount of time. Our company was due to arrive the next day. It was hours later when I received a phone call from him. He told me that he had been arrested and the car had been impounded.

I think he may have been arrested for driving while his license was suspended or something like that. He was always getting stopped for drunk driving, suspended license, or something.

It was so embarrassing to have to ask my brother and his wife to take me to get the car out of impoundment soon after they arrived the next day. They also followed me to the jail to bail my husband out so they could keep an eye on the children while I went inside.

We tried to make the most out of the time they were there visiting. We went to the zoo and did a few other things while they were there. It was good to have my family members visit. I sort of hated to see them go. Sometimes I felt so all alone without any family members nearby.

Chapter 38

I APPLIED FOR A WELFARE CHECK AND FOOD stamps while I was on maternity leave. I had to pretend that I did not know where my children's father was. He was not working again.

The money that I had been able to save from working through the agency and getting unemployment was quickly dwindling, and the welfare check was not nearly enough to pay all the household expenses.

I started looking for a job a couple of weeks after I had my daughter. I started working after four weeks. I could not afford to stay off a full six weeks. I decided to take a night shift supervisor position at a nearby nursing home, due to thinking it would be easier to secure babysitting for our three small children at night rather than during the day. I had two little girls in pampers. I also had to see to it that our six-year-old son got to and from school.

My husband kept the kids since he was not working when I went back to work. The first night shift job I had was from eleven at night until seven thirty in the morning, five days a week. It seemed to be working out well for the most part. He would usually get home in time, but when he did not, I had to make other babysitting arrangements.

Sometime later, I was offered another night shift supervisor position further away with hours from seven in the evening until seven thirty in the morning, three days per week. That made it easier for me due to not having to be away from the house as much, even though it was longer hours, and my husband would be expected to watch our children three nights per week instead of five. It was not the ideal situation, but I had to do what I had to do. Also, the benefits were better on this job.

Now my husband had to get home earlier to be with the children. He was usually good for two out of three nights at first. But one day, our son told me that his grandmother came over, and she and his father had gone down in the basement to smoke, and they would not let him come down. I was infuriated to find out they were smoking crack in the house with the children. Of course, I let my husband know in no uncertain terms that I did not appreciate them smoking crack in the house, especially with the children there.

I used to confide in an older Caucasian Christian nurse where I worked. I would tell her about different things I was going through in my marriage. I did not know a lot of scripture at that time, but I did know that the Lord hates divorce. I told her I was reluctant to leave my husband because of that. I knew that if an unbelieving husband or wife left their believing spouse that the Lord would not hold it against the believing spouse. But I also knew that my husband had no intention of leaving. One day, my coworker explained to me that my husband had already left due to his actions and his lack of commitment and provision for me and our children. I pondered on what she said.

I was really fighting a losing battle, because one of my husband's brothers had recently moved within walking distance of where we lived, and his mother and other brothers would oftentimes go there to hang out.

One evening, when I was preparing to go to work, my husband told me that he was going to walk to the corner store to get a beer before he started watching the children. He had plenty of time to get back home before I had to leave. I waited for as long as I could before having to leave so I would not be late for work. I hoped that he would be back momentarily.

When I got to work, I was on pins and needles. I hurried and took the report and called home to make sure he had arrived. There were no cell phones at that time, so I could not call on the way to work. I called two or three times and did not get an answer. I spoke with the director of nursing and told her that I had to go home to check on my children. I promised that I would come back as soon as I made sure they were okay. She granted me leave.

I could not get home fast enough. When I came through the door, my son was trying to change his baby sister's messy pamper. I guess the smell had gotten to be too much. He looked at me as if to say, "I'm trying my best, but this is too much!" Once again, I was hurt and infuriated. The least my husband could do was to watch the children while I worked. After all, he was not helping to pay any of the bills.

I was pretty sure he was nearby at his brother's house. I got in the car and drove there. He was there just as I had suspected, with his mother, his two brothers, and some other people getting high. I was so outdone. I threatened to kill him if he allowed something to happen to the children due to his negligence. He had lied to his family and told them that I did not have to work and was home with the kids.

His brother who had watched my son at times in the past offered to go to our home and watch the children that night. He was not the ideal babysitter either, but I had to get back to work. I could only hope that the others did not come to the house after I left and resume their party there.

Chapter 39

I KNEW THINGS HAD TO CHANGE QUICKLY. BUT I decided that I was not going to pay a babysitter while my husband was out of work, hanging around getting high every day, and using the house for a crack house while I was at work.

I had to be extra careful not to leave anything of value out in the open, especially since other people were coming to the house while I was away. One day, I discovered that the *Hooked on Phonics* reading material that I had bought for our son was missing. Of course, no one admitted to taking it.

The straw that broke the camel's back happened one morning when I got home from work. I had hidden the grocery money inside of a pair of socks in the back of my drawer that was full of socks. I did not want to take that much money with me to work. I never thought he would find it there. However, when I looked for the money, every penny was gone. I have heard that crack addicts can smell money. My husband had left the house when I discovered the money was gone.

I can remember closing my eyes and clutching the sides of my head with my fists. I thought I was going to lose my mind that day. I just could not take it anymore. But suddenly, I saw a bright light, brighter than any light I had ever seen before. I knew it was not a natural light. I still had my eyes closed. Then I was enveloped with a warm sensation that started from my head and went down my body. The warm sensation brought calmness and peace, and I heard the voice of the Lord say, "He is going to leave today."

My husband came back later that day, but I told him what I heard the Lord say, "You have to leave today."

He replied, "I know."

I knew it was an act of God that he agreed so readily. He left that day without a fuss. I think he went to his mother's home, or to whoever would let him stay for a day or two.

Of course, he wanted to see the children after he left. But he also wanted to keep me under his radar. Sometimes he would just show up at the door. I never wanted to keep him from seeing the children, but it would have to be a time that was not only convenient for him, but for us too. He did not take me seriously, so he would just show up sometimes anyway. I left him standing outside knocking a few times, and then he finally discovered that he really needed to call first.

However, there were a couple of times that he had gotten into the apartment through the basement window, sometime during the night when I was working. I was still working the 7:00 p.m. to 7:00 a.m. shift. I would drop my son off at school on the way home and then proceed to go home with my two daughters. It would really unnerve me when I thought we were home alone, and he would suddenly come up the basement stairs, especially since his uncle had killed his wife in a similar situation only a few months before.

I paid the leasing office to put bars on the basement windows so he could no longer get in that way.

On one occasion, he came late at night and knocked on the door. I think he had been getting high. I would not open the door, so he shattered the picture window with a brick. I told him I had called the police, and they were on their way. He left before the police arrived. It traumatized our oldest daughter who was only two and a half years old. She talked about it repeatedly to me and whoever she encountered for quite some time. Fortunately, she was not in school yet.

I did file a police report that night and attempted to get a restraining order the next day, but I was told that I could not restrain my husband from his home since he had not assaulted me. However, I think I convinced my husband that I had gotten the order, and he did not try to force his way in again.

Two or three months later, he decided to relocate to North Carolina where he had relatives. He would come back every so often to visit.

He would always threaten that I better not have another man around his kids, even though he thought it was okay to be involved with other women and their children.

Chapter 40

THE PROPHET AT MY CHURCH HAD PREVIOUSLY given me a Word from God. He prophesied that there was a distraction in my life preventing me from serving the Lord the way I wanted to. He also prophesied that the Lord was going to move the distraction out of my way, but when He did, I should commit my life totally to Him.

I wish I could say that I totally committed myself to the Lord after my husband and I separated, but unfortunately, that is not what happened. The Spirit of the Lord was in me, but I was not filled with the Spirit as I desperately needed to be. I loved the Lord, but I was not rooted and grounded in Him at this point in my life. I did not have much of a prayer life, and I did not read the Word as often as I should.

I had all sorts of mixed emotions, and I tried to manage them by myself. In a way, I felt like the weight of the world had been lifted off my shoulders, but at the same time, I knew I had a great undertaking ahead of me raising our three children alone.

I was angry that our marriage did not work out. I was angry with myself for giving my twenties to a man that did not appreciate me, marrying him, and bearing his three children. I was angry with my husband for not working with me to make our marriage work. I later came to realize that I was even angry with God for how things turned out. But He had tried to warn me.

I was able to put a smile on my face and speak in a pleasant manner to most people, but I was in desperate need of a healing—a healing that I would not experience for years to come.

I continued to go to church on Sundays, but it was difficult taking the children with me. My son and youngest daughter did fine in the sanctuary with me or in children's church, but my oldest daughter would not have any part of going to children's church, and she would not behave and be quiet in church with me. She was in her "terrible twos." On more than one occasion, the ushers would chastise me for not keeping her quiet or give me the look.

The enemy had no intention of letting me get closer to the Lord. God had a plan for me, but so did Satan. He tried to unnerve me on Sundays when I was preparing to go to church, reminding me of how my daughter had acted the previous Sunday. I knew we needed to be in church, but it became increasingly discouraging.

When the devil sets traps to ensnare us—he always sets more than one.

Chapter 41

THERE WAS A MAN ON MY JOB who worked in housekeeping. I once needed some furniture moved, and I knew he had a truck. I asked if he and another one of our coworkers could move the furniture for me. He agreed, so I gave him my number so we could coordinate a time.

He would always say nice things to me when our paths crossed on the job. On one occasion, he complemented me on how beautiful my eyes were. Hearing these kind words was very refreshing after so recently coming out of a mentally, physically, and emotionally abusive and disappointing relationship. I was vulnerable to say the least.

At first, I just thought he was just being nice. After all, he was married. But after I gave him my number, he randomly started to call me. At first, he would say he was just checking on me. He knew that my husband and I had separated. But after he found out that my husband had moved out of town, he started calling more regularly.

He started talking about getting together and going on an outing, maybe to take my son fishing. I reminded him that he was married with two children. He made it sound as if it was innocent, but I knew that doing something like that would be inappropriate. But after a while, all the attention he was giving me began to lure me in.

I was really impressed when I got off work one Saturday morning after working all night to have him flag me down and tell me that he just wanted to see me before he went to work. He was on his way to his weekend day job at the hospital.

One Sunday, I went to church, and the pastor gave a Word of warning. She called out my specific situation. She said, "There is a woman here today who is becoming attracted to a man that she should not be attracted to." She went on to make an altar call for the woman to come up and get prayer for deliverance. I knew she was talking to me, but I was too ashamed to go up to the altar. Another woman went up for prayer, so I felt a sigh of relief. But the pastor was not deceived. When I did not go up, she said, "There is someone else who should come up as well." I did not budge from my seat. Part of me was embarrassed, but another part of me really did not want to be delivered, especially not until I had a chance to partake of the forbidden fruit at least once. I would live to regret the path I took.

Chapter 42

THE SCRIPTURE SAYS IN MATTHEW 12:43–45 (NLT), "When an evil spirit leaves a person, it goes into the desert, seeking rest but finding none. Then it says, "I will return to the person I came from." So it returns and finds its former home empty, swept, and put in order. Then the spirit finds seven other spirits eviler than itself, and they all enter the person and live there. And so that person is worse off than before.

I found this scripture to be true in my case. I was not able to discern all seven of the additional evil spirits right away, but over time, I was able to identify each one of these wicked entities.

I ended up in a full-fledged relationship with this married man. Foolishly, I tried to justify what I was doing; after all, I had been cheated on by my husband. I chose to believe the lie.

It was not long before I completely stopped going to church, reading my Bible, and praying, for one thing I felt too convicted, and for another I was not ready to quit doing what I was doing.

The married man smoked marijuana and drank alcohol. I soon started to do the same. It seemed to help dull the conviction I was feeling. Although he did not smoke cigarettes, I eventually started smoking cigarettes again as well. However, one night, he lit up a cigarette laced with crack, and I adamantly refused to smoke it with him and asked him not to smoke it in my presence. I was still traumatized with how it had totally devastated my marriage. He honored that wish.

We ended up believing that we had fallen in love. But the Bible says, love is kind, does not behave rudely, does not seek its own, does not rejoice in iniquity but rejoices in truth, etc. Our relationship was the opposite of the biblical meaning of love, and I knew nothing good could come of it.

The Bible also says that love does not envy. But I felt envious when he could not come by on a holiday or he would go out of town with his family, and I was left out. I knew I did not have a right to feel that way, but I did.

After a while, I started coming down off the high this relationship had initially provided for me. I tried to get out of it, but I felt trapped. The Bible does not refer to love as being a trap.

This ungodly soul tie we had formed was not going to be easy to break. There were times when I would tell him that I wanted to stop the affair, that we never should have started it, and that I felt like the harlot that I was. I would feebly try to sever the relationship by not answering the phone when he would call, but he would keep calling or show up at the door. Trouble is easy to get into but hard to get out of.

I started going out on occasions, by myself or with a friend, trying to put some space between us, but that ended up leading me down another forbidden path.

Chapter 43

BY THE GRACE OF GOD, I WAS still caring for my children and working, but I was slipping deeper and deeper into the darkness.

One night, I decided to go out by myself. I ended up at a club I had heard about. I was sitting at the bar when a man I had never met before came up and started talking to me. He seemed nice enough, so I responded. He sat down beside me, and we talked and laughed for a while. He ended up inviting me to his motorcycle club not too far away. They kept hours later than the regular clubs. I followed him there in my car.

The party was lively, and we danced and drank the night away. The atmosphere was different. They all seemed to know and respect one another like a big happy family.

I lost track of time and almost forgot I had to work the morning shift, which was only a few short hours away. I excused myself, gave him my number, and left.

This was the beginning of another illicit affair.

We went out a few times before I came to know that he was married and that his wife was a minister. My guilt was compounded, but I kept right on going down this slippery slope. If you give the enemy an inch, he will take a mile. If you let him ride, he will drive.

I found myself in a lust triangle with both men vying for my time, energy, and body. I was in bondage, and I knew it. There was no peace in the situation that I was in, no matter how I tried to deceive myself.

The new guy did not smoke crack, but he did cocaine. I found myself on more than one occasion indulging with him.

At first, I made sure I only got high after I got off work or on my off days, but eventually I started doing a little smoking and drinking two or three hours before I was to report to work.

Thank God, I did not lose my job or my children or my mind due to my insanity. But I knew that I was headed for destruction at full speed, and I somehow had to slow down.

God warned me in different ways that judgment was coming. I felt like Jonah on the ship who was headed for Tarshish when he should have been going to Nineveh. The storm started affecting the people who I was on the ship with. On one occasion, a tree fell on the car of one of the men in my life and totaled his car. On another occasion, a deer ran out in front of his motorcycle, causing him to wreck and break his leg. Some people might have thought these things just happened, but I knew that God was using nature to give me a rude awakening. He was letting me know that if I did not start going in the right direction, I was going to become shipwrecked along with others on the ship.

One night, in the wee hours of the morning, I found myself pacing the floor and calling out to God. I had not done that in what seemed like forever. I felt so far away from Him that I really did not think He was listening to me, but He was. My breakthrough did not come suddenly, but it would come. Roman 10:13 tells us, "Everyone who calls on the name of the Lord will be saved."

Not much changed for another year or so. But God continued to speak to me, telling me that it was time for me to come back home.

Chapter 44

My children and I would drive to West Virginia every year to visit my grandparents in the summer, but they relocated to North Carolina in 1996, and we started driving down to visit them there. The trip in 1998 was different than the others. When we got back home, I kept thinking that we should move to North Carolina and that I had overstayed my welcome in Ohio. It would be the fresh start that I so desperately needed! However, I would push the thoughts away, figuring we might move sometime in the distant future.

After the New Year came in 1999, I began to think about our yearly trip to North Carolina, but the prompting to move there felt even stronger now. I started telling my children and other people that I was thinking about moving there, and it became even more real to me.

I did not have any real friends or family in Ohio, and the soul ties I had there were long overdue to be broken!

My children had family there on their father's side, but I figured we could arrange to visit them, or they could come visit us, and that did happen on several occasions.

We had not been contacted by my children's father for quite some time. I heard he was in jail. I had gotten a divorce a couple of years after we separated. It was not difficult since he had not lived in the state since shortly after we separated. However, he would come to visit from time to time.

My ex-sister-in-law asked me why I had decided to move, and my response was, "I don't know, but I feel like I have to go." It was almost as if the Lord picked me up and placed me where He wanted me to be.

Around the time that my children and I would usually go to North Carolina for our annual trip, I went there to apply for jobs and to look for housing while my children were away for a few days at summer camp. I had scheduled two job interviews at a hospital and one at a nursing home prior to traveling there. The hospital and nursing home were owned by the same organization.

The married man whom I had most recently gotten involved with offered to drive me to North Carolina.

When I got back to Ohio, I was informed that I had been accepted for all three jobs, so I chose one of the positions in the hospital. I had been a nurse for eleven years by that time.

I was turned down for one of the townhomes I really liked and had applied for, but I got accepted by another. Things were falling into place. I had a little less than a month to relocate and start my hospital orientation.

My ex-husband's family may not have been totally in agreement with my decision to move away, but my ex-mother-in-law and two of her sisters helped me pack up our things.

They insisted on helping, and none of them would accept any money for helping except for her brother who helped load the U-Haul before my married companion drove us down. When I considered how much they had all helped, I realized that we could never have gotten everything packed and ready to go in time if they had not stepped in to assist. God was orchestrating everything.

I scheduled to turn the truck in at a U-Haul company in North Carolina. My boyfriend packed his motorcycle on the truck so he could ride back after helping us to unload everything. However, he stayed the weekend before traveling back. We had planned to go to a club that Saturday night, but my family member who was supposed to go out with us was not able to make it. So we did not end up going out since we did not know where any clubs were. But we still ended up partying together, drinking, and smoking weed. I had a little over a week before my orientation was scheduled to start.

We continued to communicate after he got back to Ohio. We talked about him planning a trip back down to visit soon.

However, it was not long before he started talking about leaving his wife and two teenaged children and moving to North Carolina. I had never mentioned anything to him about leaving his wife and family. Being involved with him was bad enough. I would mostly listen when he would talk that way. Even in my backslidden condition, I knew that the best thing for us to do was to part ways for good. But soul ties are hard to break.

Chapter 45

My children and I started our "new beginning." I got my children enrolled in their new schools and did some unpacking after the weekend. I was also scheduled to take a drug test that week. I had smoked marijuana a few days before, so I went to GNC and purchased a bottle of Golden Seal so I could take some and mask my sure to be positive drug test. School for the children and my job orientation would start the following week.

We went to our family reunion in a nearby city that upcoming weekend. We had a great time! It was so good to see family members that I had not seen in a while and even some I had never seen.

The children started school that Monday. I think my orientation was scheduled to start the following Tuesday or Wednesday.

I was little nervous, but I was mostly excited about my new job. I had managed to save some money for the move, but moving always costs more than what is estimated, and I was starting to get a little low on cash. I made sure I arrived at orientation in time and found my assigned seat. They distributed the orientation packets, but I did not get one, so I informed the instructor. After verifying my name, I was called into a back room and informed that I had failed my drug test. I was so humiliated. I felt like my whole world had come crashing down! What was I going to do? I was devastated, but I had no one to blame except myself.

I drove home feeling numb. This was truly a surreal experience. I felt like crying, but the tears would not come, so I cried out to the Lord asking Him to help me find a job for me and my children just in case He chose to hear me. I had not really prayed in a long time. I had turned my back on God, but He had never stopped trying to get my attention, whether in a good way or in a not so good way.

After I prayed, I looked in the phone book for nursing jobs and started applying for new jobs. I still had some marijuana my so-called boyfriend gave me before he went back to Ohio, but I threw it in the trash. I had to get my priorities in order immediately! Even if I got a job right away, I still may not be able to pass the drug test.

It was a few weeks before I was offered another job. I was truly grateful. By this time, my cash flow had almost come to a screeching halt. I had been given a serious lesson in humility. I was especially thankful that I passed the drug test. I think I may have passed it honestly this time, but I took some Golden Seal just in case.

I had started working on my bachelor's degree and had completed several courses prior to moving from Columbus. It was a self-paced degree program, and even though I had not cared much for the mental health rotations in nursing school, I had decided to major in psychiatric nursing. Lo and behold, the job I was offered was in psychiatric nursing.

I was not only offered a registered nursing position, but I was offered a night shift supervisor position due to my previous years of supervisory experience. I did not feel prepared to supervise in an area I was still studying, but I did not have much of a choice. I had to make some money before we got evicted. Thankfully I had paid two weeks prorated rent and a full month's rent when we moved in.

Chapter 46

MY GRANDPARENTS HAD SURPRISINGLY MOVED FROM THE city they were living in in North Carolina to Greensboro just a few weeks before we moved to Greensboro. It worked out well because we would not have to drive as far to visit them. My grandmother wanted to find a new church home, and her daughter, my aunt who had also moved to Greensboro, was not able to take her to church due to working weekends. She asked if I could drive her to a couple of churches that she had been referred to. I agreed to oblige her. I was not ready to rededicate my life to the Lord, and I still wanted to party, but I could take her to church.

It had been several weeks since I had started my new job, and I had not smoked any marijuana since failing the drug test. I talked to one of my brothers who lived in Durham, North Carolina, one day, and he invited me to come and visit with him and his wife that upcoming weekend. I agreed to come on Saturday and stay until Sunday afternoon. We were supposed to go out clubbing on Saturday night.

I politely bowed out to take my grandmother to church that Sunday and left my children with my grandparents. My grandfather had become chronically ill and did not leave the house very often. My grandparents were still raising my niece, so my children had someone there around their ages.

It felt good to get away for a while. I got to my brother and sister-in-law's home on Saturday afternoon. We went out to eat and did some shopping. When we got back to their house, none of us felt much like going out, but my brother and I started drinking alcohol and smoking weed. I started feeling a little woozy, and before I knew what was happening, I was lying on the floor on my back still seated in my chair. My brother and his wife were standing over me asking me if I was okay. I knew it had been a while since I had smoked or drank anything, but nothing like this had ever happened to me before.

Regardless of what anyone else may think, I truly believed an angel of the Lord knocked me over to try to knock some sense into me. I did not want anything else to drink or smoke that night. I felt like it was another wake-up call. The Lord had blessed me with another job, and my system had been clean from marijuana for several weeks.

I spent the night with them, but instead of staying until that Sunday afternoon as I had planned, I got up around seven that morning to drive back to Greensboro. My brother and his wife bid me farewell but were not expecting me to leave so soon. My brother gave me some weed to take home with me. I was a little reluctant to take it, but I did anyway.

I could not get back fast enough! We ended up going with my grandmother to church after all. The Lord had been dealing with me, but I was still trying to run.

My grandmother really did not feel at home at the churches she had been recommended to, but we kept looking. That was the least I could do for my grandmother; after all, she had really been good to us when we were growing up, and she was my go-to whenever I needed to talk to someone.

One Sunday, we were headed back to one of the churches we had previously visited, but I could tell my grandmother was not too excited about it. There was a little church that we had passed by on

Sundays as we church hunted, and I suggested that we visit there. She agreed. We all felt welcome there, and we all enjoyed the service.

The pastor fell in love with my grandmother right away. We learned that he had been pastoring a little less than a year when we started attending the church. His father, the bishop, had become ill and could no longer lead the church. The pastor later told us that he had become discouraged and was contemplating stepping down, and that he had prayed for more church mothers and seasoned members to join the church. He said my grandmother was an answer to his prayers. He would oftentimes tell his testimony over the pulpit about how she had inspired him to hang in there.

Chapter 47

WE STARTED GOING TO CHURCH THERE EVERY Sunday, and I would feel the Holy Spirit come upon me during the services. I was still trying to resist Him, but after about six weeks, I rededicated my life to the Lord. The continual assembling of myself with the believers and the urgings and convictions of the Holy Spirit had become too much for me to resist.

On one occasion, when I got off from work in the morning and my children had gone to school, I was sitting on my bed smoking some of the weed my brother had given me. Suddenly, I could see into the spirit realm. I saw demonic figures rushing into the room, the door slammed, and my spirit was snatched from my body. I was looking down at my body sitting there on the bed. It was as if I could hear the Lord warning me that my life could end just that easily. I was very shaken up after that experience. It was the second time that I had had an out-of-body experience, and both times it was not long before I rededicated my life to the Lord.

Another morning after I had gotten home from work and was lying in bed, I decided to tune in to a Christian program, and I heard a young woman sharing her testimony. She explained how she had backslid and brought shame and reproach on her family and God. Suddenly, I started weeping uncontrollably. She was telling my story.

That morning, I cried out in repentance and asked the Lord to come back into my life, and He did. What a blessed Savior!

Jeremiah 3:14–15 says, "'Return, O backsliding children,' says, the Lord, 'for I am married to you. I will take you, one from a city and two from a family, and I will bring you to Zion. And I will give you shepherds according to My heart, who will feed you with knowledge and understanding.'"

I knew my grandmother had been praying for me, and the next time she saw me, she knew right away that I had had an encounter with the Lord. She told me that my countenance had changed.

My grandfather died within two months of us moving to North Carolina. He had never been able to attend the new church due to his medical conditions, so my grandmother got their previous pastor to perform his eulogy. However, our new pastor came to my grandfather's service. That really won my grandmother's heart.

I began to hunger and thirst after God's righteousness and found Matthew 5:6 to be true; I was being blessed and filled. I had no intention of turning my back on the Lord this time. I was sick and tired of being sick and tired of living my sinful lifestyle. I now saw myself as being married to my Redeemer, and I wanted to be a faithful wife.

During the first year after joining the church, our pastor had seasoned men and women of God that his father had fellowshipped with to come to the church and preach. I learned so much. I was like a sponge; I soaked up everything I could from them and our pastor, but I knew something was missing.

One night, a woman pastor came to preach. She really blessed my soul with how she expounded on the scriptures. I answered the altar call she made after the sermon and told her that I wanted to be filled with the Holy Spirit. She explained that the filling of the Holy Spirit is a gift that we can simply ask for. She demonstrated this as she told me to ask her for her Bible, and she in turn handed it to me. Of course, I gave her Bible back to her, but I had learned something from her that night that would help me stay connected to the Lord this time. All I had to do was ask. I was not filled with the Spirit that night with the evidence of speaking in tongues, but I continued to ask the Lord to fill me.

One morning after I got home from work during my devotional time, it seemed as though I could hear myself in the spirit speaking in tongues. It was as if the Holy Spirit told me to say what I heard and I did. The unknown language came pouring out of me like a dam that broke. I was so overjoyed; the gift of the Holy Spirit had been manifested to me, and it was not very long after I had started asking the Lord to fill me. It has been over twenty years since I was initially filled with the Holy Spirit, and I can truly say that He has been my Keeper, and I have not backslidden anymore. I have also come to know that we need to be filled continually.

During that year, our pastor also invited a bishop to come and speak at our church. He taught about ungodly soul ties and how to be delivered from them. The Lord knew I desperately needed that. For a short while after I rededicated my life to the Lord, I would still receive phone calls from both men whom I had been involved with in Columbus, but God gave me the strength to permanently break the connections with them.

I wanted to be an active member in my church and in the kingdom of God. I joined our church's outreach group. I loved to go out with the members of the group to minister in the community. I went to a shelter near my home and taught Bible study on a couple of occasions. I passed out tracks in my neighborhood. I also enrolled in a home-based Bible college to try to learn all that I could.

Toward the end of the first year at the church, our pastor informed me that God had revealed to him that I was called to be a minister of the gospel, and he ordained me a minister in training (MIT). I agreed with him as God had also revealed the calling to me in dreams, visions, and the desire to do so.

One day, some of us church members went out to eat, and one of the elders prophesied that I was going to marry a bishop. On another occasion, it was prophesied that I would be a pastor. I knew I was not ready for either of these things to take place at the time, but I held on to the words. I wanted whatever happened in my life to be in God's timing and according to His will.

I repented to my children about not having them in church during my backslidden condition and really emphasized how important it is to go to church and to form a meaningful relationship with God. They enjoyed going to church and being involved in the children's ministry.

The Lord revealed to me the spiritual gifts that He had for my children. He had me to speak over my son, that he was to be mighty in faith and that what he believed for would certainly come to pass; over my oldest daughter, that she would be a powerful prayer warrior and win many spiritual battles in the heavenlies; and over my youngest daughter, that she would be a discerning prophetess and that whatever she spoke would not fall to the ground unfulfilled. I still believe that His promises will be manifested in their lives.

Later, the pastor and his wife talked with me about starting a single mother's ministry at the church. She told me that she had been over the single mother's ministry at her previous church. I agreed to do so, but not really knowing what was expected, it took me a while to get started. But once I did, I had monthly meetings, I invited a male nurse whom I worked with who was also a martial arts teacher to come out and show them some moves during one of the meetings, and once I invited the women and their children over to our home for a cookout.

Chapter 48

I CONTINUED TO WORK AT THE BEHAVIORAL HEALTH center, and God allowed me to see some demonic activities that are oftentimes involved with mental illnesses. The experiences caused me to develop a consistent prayer life.

On one occasion, one of the female patients came to the medication room to ask for her asthma inhaler. I gave it to her. She began to speak about her mental illness as if to glorify it. She explained that she and her sister were diagnosed with mental illness. Normally, I would have just listened and offered words of empathy, but I felt prompted by the Holy Spirit to speak to her about how Jesus had bled, suffered, and died so we could be healed from those types of illnesses. Suddenly, I saw her face transform into a lion's face, and her voice sounded like a lion's would if it could talk. She roared, "Why do you have to talk about Jesus?" I felt the hairs stand up on the back of my neck, and I felt like running, but the Holy Spirit urged me to stand still and continue to talk about Jesus. She threw her inhaler on the top of the medication cart and ran down the hall to her room. She would not even look in my direction the next morning when they were lining up for breakfast.

Another night, a man was admitted proclaiming he was God and the king of the universe. He ranted and raved off and on the whole night. I could tell it was demons speaking through him, and I could feel their presence. The Lord prompted me to fast and pray for him after I left work. When I came back to work that night, he was quiet and seemed to be in his right mind.

While working on the children's unit, I would see little children acting out with the strength of men, requiring several staff members to restrain them. I saw one boy transform into what appeared to be a pixie-like form, pointed ears and all. I saw another small child scale a bookshelf with the speed and agility of a monkey.

The spirit of suicide and self-harm ran rampant in the hospital population. Many times, adults and children cut themselves with knives or razors prior to being admitted, saying it was a way to relieve the mental pain they felt. Frequently their cuts were on their wrists, and sometimes they were deep, requiring bandaging.

One day, I woke up to find that I had a few very fine superficial scratches on my inner wrist as if caused by something very sharp. I could not figure out how they occurred. I ended up shrugging it off, knowing that I am a bit accident-prone. However, when it occurred again and again, it was obvious that it was not an accident. It became apparent that the superficial wounds were being inflicted supernaturally while I was sleeping.

Even though the scratches were very light and superficial and did not bleed, they developed scabs, and by me being black, the scars that remained after the areas healed turned dark and became very noticeable. I tried to cover my wrist area to prevent people from seeing them. However, one day, one of the other nurses on my unit saw them and asked about them. All I could answer was, "You do not want to know."

I had to really go into major spiritual warfare, announcing to the demonic force(s) that my soul, body, and spirit belong to the Lord and they had no right to any part of me. That worked, and they were no longer able to inflict the wounds.

These are just a few of the things that I experienced there, and God began to teach me firsthand about demonic activity, spiritual warfare, and deliverance.

Chapter 49

G OD SHOWED ME THAT "THERE IS NO good thing that He will withhold from them that walk uprightly" (Psalm 84:11).

I had only been working at the behavioral health hospital for five months when it was announced that the facility was being shut down. When I first started working there, I had no knowledge of the fact that some of their other facilities had been closed due to reports of abuse and neglect. However, over the course of time, I heard things from the staff and from a family member in the community about their history. There were rumors that our facility was also going to be closed, but the leadership denied it.

One day, all the staff were called to a meeting, and we were informed that our facility would be closing in a matter of days. We all scattered to find work. I applied for and was hired for a position that I was referred to by one of my coworkers at a jail in a city about thirty minutes from where we lived. It was not my ideal job, but I felt I could not be picky under the circumstances.

I had only been in orientation for a couple of days at the jail when I got a call from a previous leader from the mental health center. I was asked if I would be interested in being one of the staff they needed to watch over the building at night while it was being renovated during the day for the new owners. They also wanted a nurse on board to triage any calls that came in needing to be referred to other places or services. There were no longer any patients there, and I was offered a salary significantly higher than I was being offered at the jail. I accepted the offer, and the fact that it was closer to home was an extra bonus. God gave me favor, as I had less seniority than the other nurses who had worked there. One of them should have been called back instead of me, but God!

After they finished the renovations at the facility, the new owners called some of the previous staff members to work for them, and thank God I was in the number. However, I discovered that the new owners were the owners of the hospital chain that I had applied with and been hired by before I moved to North Carolina. They had a policy that if anyone failed a drug test with them, the individual had to wait six months before they could apply again.

It had not been quite six months since I failed their drug test. But thanks to God's perfect timing, the onboarding process took a little longer than expected, and I was one day past the six-month mark when I was scheduled to take the drug test. Even the person who drew my blood made a comment about the close timeline. Hallelujah! Thank God for His amazing, abundant, and abounding grace!

I was made aware a few months later that some of the staff who had worked for the previous owners filed a lawsuit over how the layoff was handled, and we ended up getting a considerable amount of money through the class action suit. Blessings on blessings!

The Lord blessed my children and I with a brand-new house while I was working there. I would oftentimes get off work in the morning and go to the building site to see how much further they had gotten on the building project. By faith, I would walk on the land praying and pronouncing affirmations that the builders would build the house with the spirit of excellency and that no weapons formed against us to be able to get the house would prosper.

I worked at the new behavioral health center for three years. I probably would have worked there longer, but I felt that the Lord was telling me that I needed to find a day shift job, since my children were getting older. I did not need any adolescent problems to develop while I was away working at night.

I had to step out on faith. I had been promoted back to my previous supervisor position, gotten generous raises each year, and was paid night shift differential. I would have to take a significant pay cut almost anywhere else I went to work.

I signed up with some nursing agencies and gave my notice. It was not a smooth transition. Sometimes, the agencies would schedule shifts and then cancel them at the last minute. At other times, they would call me at the last minute to fill a shift. I had to make a certain amount of money every month to pay the mortgage, all the other bills, and buy food. But during my transition, the Lord blessed me so that I did not miss a mortgage payment. Until this day, I cannot figure out in my head how I was able to do all of that. God wanted to teach me a lesson from Isaiah 1:19: "If you are willing and obedient, you shall eat the good of the land."

It took six months for me to find a full-time day shift job, according to the specifications that I believed the Lord gave me: I would have to have Sundays off and one day off during the week. My new manager agreed to give me weekends off and one day off during the week. She said the job required staff to work forty hours per week, so she scheduled me to work four ten-hour shifts. The Lord did exceedingly, abundantly above all that I asked or thought (Ephesians 3:20).

Chapter 50

Not long after I secured my new job in December 2003, I started feeling restless and somewhat uncomfortable at our church. I tried to push the feelings away, but they continued to reoccur. I had been ordained as a minister in training, but we were not having any ministry training. I was called on to minister from time to time and to teach Sunday School for a while, but I still felt like something was missing. After a while of wrestling with what I should do, I gave the pastor my notice and started looking for a new church home. Until this day, I do not know if it was the Lord, the flesh, or the devil that directed me to leave. No matter how spiritual we may think we are, sometimes we do miss God.

I no longer needed to transport my grandmother to church. During the year, one of my aunts and an uncle had moved from the states where they lived to be closer to my grandmother and had started coming to the church. My aunt who previously had to work Sundays was now getting Sundays off and started coming to church as well.

My grandmother had started to become more and more forgetful and was living alone. My grandfather had died a few years earlier, and my niece who my grandparents were raising had gone to live with my sister, her mother, in Florida the year before.

The next year on Mother's Day, I decided to attend church with my grandmother and other family members and then go out to eat with them after church.

My two daughters and I sat near the back of the church as the church was crowded when we got there. Unfortunately, my son was not able to come due to having to work. He had started working part-time at a restaurant near our home right before his fifteenth birthday. The only sneakers he started wanting to wear far exceeded my budget, so we agreed that it was time for him to get a job.

During the service, there was a man seated on the first pew of the church in the row next to us, who kept looking back at me. After about the third time of seeing him looking back, I looked at him as if to ask, "Why do you keep looking back at me?" He smiled and turned back around, but he still looked back at least a couple more times after that. During the offering, I saw the pastor call him over and whisper something to him while glancing back at me.

After the service, my children and I surprised my grandmother by letting her know that we were there and decided with the family what restaurant we were going to meet at to celebrate Mother's Day.

When my children and I got to my car, the man who kept looking back at me in church came up to me before I had a chance to get in the car and announced, "God told me you are going to be my wife." I quickly got into my car and closed the door, not knowing what to say back to him. I had never seen him before. He was not attending the church when I left. He walked away, but before I could pull out of the parking lot, the pastor came up to my car. I told him what the man had said to me. He told me that the man had been at the church for a while, and he had gotten to know him as a man of God and an anointed prophet. He suggested that we go out to eat with him and his wife so they could officially introduce us to one another. I agreed to have his wife call me, but I was out of sorts for the rest of the day. I could not believe that a total stranger had walked up to me and said that.

The pastor's wife called me within a day or two to set up the meeting. She made it a point to tell me that it was her husband's idea for us to get together and not hers. I wondered briefly why she made it a point to tell me that, but I brushed it off. I was later told by someone in the ministry that the pastor's wife had another single mother at the church in mind for the prophet and had informed the woman that she believed he was her secret admirer. However, at the time, I was not aware of any of that and agreed to meet with them.

At an earlier time, I had discussed with someone the possibility of being married again, but I can remember telling them that God would have to tell me Himself for me to seriously consider it. Subconsciously, I thought that the prophet telling me God told him I was going to be his wife was God's way of telling me. I had come to know that the Lord works in mysterious ways, and after all, I had not ruled out being married again, and the pastor said he was a man of God. I had never been in a relationship with a man of God.

The first couple of times we scheduled to meet, there ended up being a scheduling conflict with one or more of the parties. Then she called and told me that we would have to wait, to reschedule, because the prophet had informed them that he would be going out of town for a while. Curiosity got the best of me, so I ended up asking the pastor's wife for his number.

I got up the courage to call him one day soon thereafter. When I called, he informed me that he was from Texas and that he was enroute driving there to visit. He told me that he was an ordained prophet and was planning to preach at a few churches while he was there. We talked frequently while he was out of town and began to tell each other about our past and present lives.

I told him that I was a registered nurse and worked with people who had mental health diagnoses.

He told me that he was working part-time for FedEx and ConvaTec supply company. He also told me that he was helping to manage a men's halfway house and was supposed to be put on salary soon by the owner. He said the owner was still trying to get the necessary papers together to hire someone. I later went with him a couple of times when he held Bible studies there.

He told me that he had been married twice before and that he had a daughter by his first wife and a son and daughter by his second wife. He also told me that he had been addicted to crack for fourteen years before giving his life to Christ. He explained that his crack addiction had ruined his second marriage.

I told him about being married twice before myself and being a single mother of a son and two daughters and that my ex-husband had been addicted to crack for years.

I told him how I had rededicated my life to the Lord a few years earlier and had been ordained as a minister in training and been active in the church that he was currently attending. I explained that I had left the church the previous year and had joined another church.

We both told each other about our love for ministry, and he told me that he was planning to become a pastor. I was beginning to feel that maybe this relationship was ordained by God.

I told him who my grandmother and other family members were in the ministry. I came to know that my grandmother had already met him and had a couple of brief conversations with him and thought very highly of him. That was a plus.

Chapter 51

BY THE TIME THE PROPHET GOT BACK to Greensboro, I felt like a practically knew him even though I had never spent time with him in person. I invited him over for a cookout the following weekend. I introduced him to my children as the man whom I met at grandma's church. We talked, laughed, ate, and had a nice time. My son and my oldest daughter talked freely with him; they had previously told me that they thought I should have a man in my life, since their father and I had been apart for so long. But my youngest daughter was a little reserved. She didn't want to have to share her time with me with anyone else.

He and I both had busy schedules during the week, but we continued to talk on the phone frequently, still getting to know each other.

A red flag for me was when he began to talk sexually not long after we met. I told him that I felt that talk like that was inappropriate for unmarried Christians, and if he continued to talk that way, I would no longer conversate with him. I explained that I planned to remain celibate until after I was married this time. He would stop talking like that way for a while, but would end up starting back. I would hang up and refuse to talk to him, but he would call until I answered. He even showed up at my job unexpectedly one day and brought me flowers.

Another red flag was when he later told me that instead of being married twice before, he had been married three times, and though he and his last wife were separated, they were not divorced. He told me that she had left him and moved back to Massachusetts, where she was originally from.

I felt betrayed. He had deliberately neglected to tell me about his current marriage. I wish I could say that I told him I would no longer see him until he got a divorce, but that is not what I did.

He told me the only reason he had not divorced her was because their separation had not quite been a year ago, but as soon as the year was up, he was getting a divorce.

He said they met while he was still living in Texas through a church mother whom he had grown close to after he and his second wife divorced. He explained that she and the church mother would pray and minister to one another over the phone, and he began to join in on the calls. He said she was pastoring a church in Greensboro, and after a while, they decided that he should make a fresh start, by moving to Greensboro to help her with the church.

He told me that they pastored the church together for a while, and then they decided to get married. He said he was the assistant pastor. Later they moved to Texas and pastored a church there.

He said she ended up destroying both churches due to her jealousy over his anointing and how the members preferred him over her. He said she told lies about him to the members, and on one occasion, she even called the police on him during a church service, because he would not do something she wanted him to do.

He explained, they ended up moving back to Greensboro after the church failed in Texas. He said she wanted them to start another church after they returned, but he refused to do so, and soon after that, she left him.

He painted her out to be an evil vindictive person. He said she had quit a good-paying job and hadn't worked for a while and that she had just gotten another job shortly before she left. He explained that she left him with overdue bills, which she had promised to help pay when she got her paycheck, but instead she left, and she took their car. I found myself feeling sorry for him.

I believed as I believe now that two people who love the Lord should be able to have a successful marriage, that is if it is done the way the Lord instructs in His Word. But no matter how I empathized with him, I was not totally convinced that we should get married.

He later dropped another bombshell on me. He told me that he and his latest wife attended another church in Greensboro before they separated. He said, after they separated, some of the members found out what happened, and one of the women in the church befriended him. He explained that she had assisted him by selling him a car with low monthly payments and had bought him a couple of suits. He assured me that nothing had gone on between them. Sometime later, he left that church and started going to the current church.

He said he had made some payments on the car but had fallen behind a couple of months due to not being given as many hours on his second job as he had been given previously. He said she was demanding the car back. He would not have any transportation, so I offered to loan him one thousand dollars to put down on a car that a man was selling for eighteen hundred dollars. I told him he could pay me back as little as fifty dollars a month until he could afford to pay more.

He told me that the woman had also helped him obtain a phone by adding him to her phone plan. He said she looked at the billing statement and saw that he was making numerous calls to a particular number (my number), and it had greatly increased the monthly bills. She had him removed from her phone plan. In those days, all the cell phone plans had a certain number of minutes that could be used before they started charging a phenomenal amount for any additional minutes used. Due to his credit score, he was not able to get a phone on his own.

I had never owned a cell phone and had been using the cell phone that belonged to my employer to talk to him when I was away from home. I had previously heard my manager reprimand some of my coworkers about exceeding the allotted minutes on their company phones, but I had never talked very much on mine. However, after I started talking to him, she ended up reprimanding me for using more minutes than I should have. I explained to him that we would have to talk less on the cell phone and more after I got home on my landline. It was not hard to talk to him while I was at work due to the drive time between my home visits with my clients.

I hadn't planned on getting a cell phone, but due to his dilemma and the difficulty in trying not to talk to him as much at work, I decided to apply for cell phones. He agreed to pay for a portion of the bill.

To save money, he also decided to move out of the apartment that he and his wife had rented together and move into the men's home that he was overseeing.

Later, he told me that the woman came to the church he was currently attending and told the pastor that he had gotten her pregnant. He totally denied it. He said they had never been intimate, and she had just said it out of bitterness. He said he had never led her on, but she must have thought they were going to end up getting together. He said she was very overweight and was not his type. I didn't know if he was trying to be transparent or if he wanted to make sure I heard about it from him instead of someone else.

He was very convincing, and I chose to believe him. Looking back now, I feel like one of the *silly women* that Paul talks about in 2 Timothy chapter 3.

It wasn't too long after that that he wanted to go looking for wedding rings and a wedding dress. Reluctantly, I agreed to go. After all, it did not mean that we had to get married if we decided not to do so.

We picked out the wedding rings and dress together. He chose the colors that would be worn at the wedding. I did not think that I should wear a white wedding dress, but he insisted.

My husband-to-be and his wife divorced as planned after they had been separated for a year. I started to wear my engagement ring after the divorce was finalized, even though I wasn't fully on board with us getting married. I didn't feel like I loved him enough.

In hindsight, it was too soon to be planning our wedding. I was the woman on the rebound, and he had not had time to heal from his previous marriages. I later found that I was not totally healed from my previous relationships either.

Chapter 52

WE CONTINUED TO GO TO SEPARATE CHURCHES for a few months, but he persuaded me to rejoin the church so we could attend services at the same location.

Not long after I rejoined, we met with the pastor and his wife and discussed our marriage plans. They agreed to perform our ceremony but wanted us to attend premarital counseling first. We agreed to do so.

They told us that once we were married and sat under their leadership for a while, they would like for us to branch out and pastor our own church. They knew about his desire to become a pastor and his background of having been a copastor.

I wish I could say that everything went smoothly from the time we met in their office until the time we got married, but that's not how it happened. There would be some obstacles to overcome before the big event.

One Sunday morning before one of our church services, the woman whom I was told the pastor's wife previously tried to fix up with the prophet came and sat down next to me. She was one of the single mothers in the church and had come to a few of the single mother's meetings that I had held. She informed me that my fiancé called her frequently and that she told him that he should not be calling her like that since he is engaged. She informed me that she had also told the pastor's wife about the frequent calls. She said the pastor's wife warned her that if the calls did not stop, she was going to tell me about it. I said something like, "Oh, okay," and she went to sit in another area of the church. Of course, I couldn't wait until the service was over so I could ask him about it. He had sat in the minster's section during the service, so I told him after the service that I had something to talk to him about.

He came over to visit that afternoon, and I told him what she had said. He denied calling to speak to her. He explained that whenever he called, he called to speak with her son. I knew he had been having meetings with the male youth in the ministry, so I sort of believed him. I believed him even more when he called and put her on the speaker and told her that he was engaged to be married, and he did not have any romantic interest in her.

On another occasion, the pastor and his wife called me and my husband-to-be into their office. There were two other women in the office as well. One of them I knew, but I didn't remember ever seeing the other one. The woman that I knew said the other woman accused my fiancé of telling her the same thing he had told to me, that the Lord said she was going to be his wife. I was so outdone. I hated to be mixed up in drama, especially in church. But it was obvious to see that the accuser had some mental issues. My fiancé got very upset and denied ever telling her that. I didn't believe that he had said that to her, but what made her say it?

Another obstacle was that we argued about any and everything. Our conversations would start out fine but would end up in full-blown heated discussions. If we were discussing a topic and I would say something like, "Not only that, but..." he would take it as if I was disagreeing with him, and he was not having that. Out of sheer exhaustion, I would usually end up telling him that we were essentially saying the same thing only in a different way, but not soon enough, I had to try to make my point first.

Once again, I was getting ready to marry someone with my father's mentality and the male chauvinism to boot. And I, like my mother, did not back down easily.

We talked about our disagreements in our premarital counseling sessions, and I would love to say that we resolved the issue, but we never did.

I would also love to say that we remained celibate premaritally, but I wouldn't be telling the truth. We fell several times before we reached the altar. Of course, I repented after each time, but I resented the fact that I had to repent in the first place. I resented him for being so persistent and resented myself for being weak. I truly wanted to wait. He tried to convince me that there was nothing wrong with it, because we were already engaged to be married. But inside, I knew that it still wasn't right.

We were married one year and one month after we met; June 11, 2005. It was a beautiful wedding. The pastor's wife was our wedding planner, and we hired the twins who were members of the church to decorate for us. My husband's mother and one of his sisters came from Texas to attend. My grandmother was the flower girl; she was so cute. One of my aunt's was my maid of honor, and my other aunt, my daughters, and my sister-in-law were my bridesmaids. Two of my brothers were the groomsmen, along with the pastor's son and the woman's son who accused my fiancé of calling her too much. He was a teenaged boy and had always been very respectable. He had sort of bonded with my husband through the youth ministry, and he asked if he could be a part of the wedding party, and we agreed to it. My uncle and his wife lit the unity candles before the ceremony.

Unfortunately, I could not say that I was in love with the man that I was marrying, and I really didn't feel that he was in love with me. We said we loved each other, and we had convinced ourselves that it was the right thing to do. I was determined to make it work, and he said leaving was not an option for him. But we had an enormous battle ahead of us! We were two broken people, but we loved the Lord.

Chapter 53

WE WENT ON A CRUISE TO THE Bahamas for our honeymoon. Neither of us had ever been on a cruise before, and we had a nice time. We stopped in Fort Lauderdale for a couple of days and spent some time with some of my family members before heading back home.

On the way back to North Carolina, my husband got a call from his boss letting him know that he was being laid off. The news was a little unnerving seeing that we were heading back to start a home together. He had not been working there for very long. I had no desire to end up taking care of this husband like I ended up doing off and on with my previous husband!

He assured me that it would not take long for him to find another job, and I tried to be optimistic.

He had stopped working part-time for FedEx not long after we met. I think he may have been laid off or it may have been too much for him after a while.

He was fired from his previous full-time job. He said it was due to talking on the phone too much. He said he had been reprimanded for talking on the phone when he should have been working previously, and then he was caught in the restroom talking on his phone again and was fired. I was really annoyed when he told me that. I didn't care if it was me or someone else that he was talking to, it wasn't worth losing his job over.

He had moved out of the halfway house that he had been managing some time before we got married. He said the owner had never put him on salary, as promised. He rented a couple of rooms from individuals after that, but something did not suit him each time, so he moved out. He had been living in the Salvation Army's homeless shelter for a short time before we got married. We agreed that it was no need for him to look for an apartment since we were getting married soon. During one of his transitions, he asked if he could move in with us, but I told him he could not move in prior to us getting married.

Chapter 54

MY HUSBAND LOOKED FOR JOBS AFTER WE got back from our honeymoon. He drew unemployment and found some temporary agency jobs, until he could find a regular full-time job. He paid what he could toward the household expenses.

Soon after we were married, he started talking about starting our own church. I resisted at first, thinking it was much too soon. But he continuously complained of things not being satisfactory to him at our current church.

He scheduled meetings with the pastor and his wife, to discuss how to go about starting a church, and they gave us the information he requested. He had been the copastor of the other churches, so he had never completed the necessary steps to getting them up and running. The pastor had previously talked to us about wanting us to branch out from them and start a church and they would be our overseers, but I knew they were not ready for us to leave so soon.

My husband was anxious to start the church, and he was not willing to wait much longer. I stopped trying to convince him to wait after I had a dream one night about God calling us to be watchmen on the wall to warn His people as He had done with Ezekiel in Ezekiel chapter 33. I was still somewhat reluctant, but we left and started our own church three months after we were married.

My husband talked with another pastor, and he agreed to share his church space with us. There were only a handful of us at first. My daughters and a few other people who had met him through his local weekly television broadcast, *Let's Talk God*. My youngest aunt, her husband, and her daughter joined the church after a month or two. They had once belonged to our previous church, but they had stopped attending before I rejoined.

My older aunt and my grandmother still belonged to our previous church, and they visited a few times when they were not having service.

The woman from our previous church who accused my husband of calling her too much also came occasionally with her son, but they were also still members at our previous church. It was one thing for my relatives to visit, but it was a little different for other members from our previous church to come. I verbalized my concerns to my husband, but he told me he could not stop them from coming if they wanted to come. She did act respectfully when she came. She also called and asked me to pick her and her son up for church a time or two when her car was not running, so I did.

My aunt and daughters started a praise team. My aunt's daughter played the keyboard. Things seemed to be coming together.

About three months after starting the church, we found out that the woman who accused my husband of calling her too much was going back to our previous church spreading lies. She apparently told the pastor's wife that my husband had never stopped calling her and had even called her when we were on our honeymoon. She also said he had been picking her and her son up and bringing them to our church. I knew that was a lie; he had never picked them up and brought them to church. I was the one who had done that.

We also heard that the pastor had a meeting with his congregation and told them that we did not leave their church in a proper manner and the members should not be visiting our church, especially considering the woman's accusations. This caused division between us and some of my extended family members as they really did not know what to believe concerning my husband and the woman and why we had left the church so abruptly. Granted, we left before the pastor would have had us to, but my husband had talked to him about wanting to start a church and had received information from him and his wife for him to do so.

I really felt humiliated and discouraged by it all. I hated the drama. Apparently, the woman had only come to our church so she could go back and sow discord and division. My husband asked her not to come back to our church. He also said he was going to talk to the pastor and iron things out, but I did not go with him. I just wanted it to be over. A part of me blamed my husband for how things happened.

My aunt, her husband, and my cousin continued to attend our church. They said they knew the woman was lying, and they believed the Lord had led us to start the church.

Chapter 55

My husband and I had met, gotten married, started a church, and blended our family, all in sixteen months. In hindsight, I realize that was way too much, way too fast! I feel like we should have taken more time to get to know each other and to blend our family before starting the church, especially since we were both working. We did not have much quality or quantity time to spend together.

Sometimes I felt like I was the rope in a battle of tug-of-war. When an issue would arise at home, my husband wanted me to choose his side over my children's, and my children wanted me to choose their side over my husband's. Of course, I wanted to form a united front with my husband, but sometimes I felt that he should give a little.

It had been years since my husband had lived with children every day. His children were teenagers like mine, but he had not lived with them since they were small when he and their mother had separated. Besides, my children were not his biological children.

I decided to start having family meetings so we could all talk about whatever the issue was at hand and try to resolve them together. Sometimes, it worked.

By the beginning of the next year, we had enough members and had saved enough money to rent our own building. We enjoyed decorating the new sanctuary and making it our own. I helped when I could, but I was working full-time. My husband had more avail-abilities because he had not found permanent full-time employment. A few of the members were also able to help.

My husband felt that he should upgrade from the Thunderbird that he had been driving to a Cadillac. I cosigned on the loan so he could get one. I was reluctant to do so as I was a stickler about my credit ratings and I realized that he was not so much. He promised he would make sure the payments were made on time.

One thing I had gotten from the teachings at our previous church before I met him was to make sure to know about the person we were planning to marry. So before we were married, I insisted that he get a credit check, a criminal background check, and checked for sexually transmitted diseases. He agreed to do so if I would do so as well. I did not have a problem doing so. Everything came back okay, except for his credit score; it was super low, but I knew he could bring it up over time if he tried.

My husband was a very social person, especially with the mem-bers. I did not have a problem with it initially. I was aware that pas-tors should communicate with their members. I also communicated with them, but not nearly as much. Our ministry was still relatively small, and we were able to minister to our members and pray for them individually during the services.

Most of our members were female as I have found it to be in most churches that I have attended. My husband would tell me about some of the conversations that he had with certain members. Some things he shared with me I did not feel was appropriate for a pastor to discuss with the members. For instance, one of our Caucasian members shared with him that she and her husband had not slept together for over five years and that she had been sexually involved with a black man in the past.

Frequently, we would get into very heated discussions about his relationship with some of the members. During some of those heated discussions, he would tell me something that the members had said negatively about me, and that would make matters worse.

I always tried to treat everyone with kindness and respect, but he was painting me out to be someone different. He would talk down to me and try to make me feel like I was a spiritual dwarf and was only responding the way I was because I was jealous of his anointing and his relationship with the members. This is exactly what he had said about his previous wife, but now I was wondering if it was her or him.

I constantly prayed and asked the Lord if what he was saying about me was true. I did not want to be the jealous preacher's wife. I knew the church could not prosper if that was who I was. I tried to empathize, but I could not imagine sharing some of those things with any of my previous pastors or talking to the pastor negatively about his wife.

Regardless of our discussions at home, I continued to treat the members with dignity and respect.

Chapter 56

MY HUSBAND WAS STILL PAYING A NOMINAL amount towards the bill. I also found out that he had stopped making payments on my wedding ring. I refused to pay for my own wedding ring in this marriage. I had done so in my previous marriage, and I really felt like it was a deal breaker. He continued to work temporary jobs through the agencies, but they would oftentimes end abruptly, and he would have to file for unemployment. He wanted to go into full-time ministry, but there was no way he could do it at that time; the offerings were not that much. However, he did make sure that his monthly car payment was paid out of the church account.

One month, our cell phone bill more than doubled. I could not understand what happened. I had never really looked through the whole monthly statement before because the amount was always about the same. I had to find out what made the bill go up so high all of a sudden. We were still on the minutes per month plan, and the overages were phenomenal.

As I scanned through the transactions, I kept seeing the same number that had been called by my husband or had called my husband's number. There were numerous calls daily and length of some of the conversations were over an hour, and some of them were late at night. I recognized the number right away. It belonged to the same female member who had shared the inappropriate sexual information with my husband.

He had also visited her home at times while I was at work. He had explained that he had gone there to minister to her family or concerning other church matters. She was also going to give him an old Jaguar that was not in running condition, but I did not want him to bring a car to the house that was not in working order, just to sit there. He could not afford to get it fixed. She had a husband, but I wondered if he had been home during the visits or if he knew they were talking that much, or if he even cared. Her husband had been accused of molesting some of the family members.

I approached my husband about the calls initially, but of course, he played it down and even accused me of being insecure. But he was not able to convince me that I was in the wrong. I also planned to confront the woman concerning the calls.

One evening, I discovered that she and my aunt were at the church painting. I decided to go there and to take the phone bill with me to substantiate my complaint. When I arrived, I let her know that I did not appreciate the overabundance of conversations that she and my husband were having, and that I thought it was very disrespectful and inappropriate. I had never heard of a pastor talking with a member that much, especially a female member. She did not have much to say, except that he called her as much as she called him.

I later heard that my aunt had also accused me of being insecure and that I should know that my husband would not choose this unattractive woman over me. It did not matter to me how she looked, I still believed that the multitude of phone calls were disrespectful and inappropriate and had a hidden agenda. I now believed that he had probably been calling the woman at our previous church frequently, like she had said.

We later changed our cell phone carrier, and the calls and texts were not visible on the statements. It was better for me—out of sight, out of mind. The phone companies also started offering unlimited calling, so the bills would stay the same from month to month.

We had many arguments about the way he interacted with the members. He let me know with no uncertainty that he was not going to change. He would make me out to be the villain, and no matter what the discussion was about, he would play the dozen and bad-mouth my children and other family members.

During the first two to three years of our marriage, there were several times when the fights became physical. I would become so infuriated with him that I would attack him, and he would proceed to get me off of him. Sometimes these scuffles would cause some degree of injury to one or both of us. I really had to pray hard and ask the Lord to help me not to get so mad that I would strike out physically, and He did. But the arguments continued.

I knew God was not pleased with what was going on in our marriage. I could sense Him warning me at times that if we did not get things right at home, He was not going to continue to use us in ministry together.

Chapter 57

I MINISTERED ONE SUNDAY AND ONE WEDNESDAY OF every month. I would study for hours after work and on the weekends preparing for my messages. I took heed to the scripture that Paul wrote to his spiritual son in 2 Timothy 2:15: "Study to shew thyself approved unto God, a workman that needeth not to be ashamed, rightly dividing the word of truth." However, many times my husband would stand before the congregation and make comments about the message I had delivered to make them think I did not know what I was talking about, either the same day or sometime in the near future. I really felt like they were demonic attacks, but my husband was allowing himself to be used.

I would remain quiet and would not cause a scene in church, so I would wait until we got home and ask him about the comments he had made, but it would just cause another argument.

He would also criticize me for not preaching the way he did. When he preaches, he has the congregation to high-five each other and tell their neighbor one thing or the other throughout the sermon. I on the other hand am a passionate teacher, but I rarely ask the congregation to do or say anything. I tried to explain to him that I had to preach the way the Lord wanted me to preach. Otherwise, I would feel like a phony.

I did not trust him, and I certainly did not think he had my best interest at heart. Occasionally, things that he had said about me to the members would get back to me, and I would know from conversations that we had had at home that it was true. I even heard after-the-fact that some members had left the church because of the way he treated me.

Being a first lady can be very lonely. I felt that I had no one to talk to. I did not want to air out our dirty laundry with my family members, and definitely not with the church members. I also felt that other first ladies would judge me if I spoke to them about our issues. But I have since come to realize that many pastors and first ladies feel isolated and alone, especially if Satan has convinced them that their enemy is their spouse. The struggle is real.

Chapter 58

BEFORE WE WERE MARRIED, MY HUSBAND WOULD come over on Saturdays while my children and I were cleaning the house, and he would offer to vacuum the floor or do something to help out, but after we were married, he would not do any chores. Even after my children left home, and it was only the two of us, he would not lift a finger to assist with anything that needed to be done in the house. However, he would on occasion cook a shrimp and fish dinner when he had a taste for it. He would also mow the lawn during the spring and summer months, but the inside chores needed to be done on a daily basis. We both were working, but I frequently had to work overtime and would get home much later than he did. I would oftentimes come home from work exhausted and still be expected to cook and clean, while he lay on the couch relaxing and watching television.

One day we had a discussion about household responsibilities with one of our older married church mothers. He told her that he refused to help me do chores. That was pretty hurtful, especially since I was washing his clothes and cleaning up after him. After he told her that, I told him that I would continue to do all the other chores, but I was no longer going to wash his clothes. I know this may sound trivial, but after all that we had been through, it felt like this was just another way of him showing me that he really did not care about me. He resented the fact that I refused to continue to wash his clothes. He told me on several occasions.

Before we were married, I had discussed with my husband-to-be that when my children were older, I wanted them to have the house that God had blessed us with and that I would like for me and him to get a house together. He agreed with what I said at the time, but many times over the years, he made it clear that he was not in agreement. He would accuse me of choosing my children over him. He would also try to shame me by telling me that the men that he worked with agreed that I should have his name put on the deed to the house. I refused to do so and reminded him of our original agreement. Once, we did look into buying a house, but the lenders said his credit score was too low. He never worked on getting his credit score up; instead, he threatened that he would make me sell the house and give him half of the money. He ended up saying that my refusal to put his name on the deed was the main reason for wanting to end the marriage.

The marriage continued to deteriorate. It got so we would communicate with each other minimally at home and at church. I felt that it annoyed him if I said anything to him at home, and if he said anything to me, it was usually something negative. Sometimes, he would actually ignore me if I said something to him at church. It was very embarrassing. It was obvious that the members knew our marriage was in shambles.

I also felt that he had his eye on another one of the female members. Even though they did not communicate with each other openly at church, their body language and eye contact did not leave much to the imagination.

We had tried to hold things together for ten years. My last-ditch effort was when we went to Florida for our tenth anniversary. I prayed that if there was any way to salvage our marriage that we would begin the process while we were away. However, I could tell that he was very distracted while we were away, and he would frequently get by himself so he could talk on the phone.

A week after we returned from our trip, we had a disagreement and decided to separate. He told me he was not interested in marriage counseling. We had discussed getting counseling before, but he would say he did not think we needed it, or he would suggest someone to counsel us who he knew prior to us getting married, and I felt they would show partiality toward him.

The last Sunday that I attended our church, I made an announcement to the congregation letting them know that we had decided to separate and I would no longer be going to church there. I told them that my husband and I had worked on jobs and in the ministry, but we had not worked on our marriage.

Several of the members cried, and so did I. I really felt remorseful for having failed the members and God this way. I later heard that he had questioned some of the members as to the reason they were crying. Apparently, they were members whom he thought he had poisoned their minds against me to the point that they would not care if I left.

After we separated, I still felt sure that my husband was involved with one of the church members. As a form of closure, I called the phone company and ordered a copy of the phone transactions. A brief review confirmed my suspicions. The same old pattern was there. There was a multitude of phone calls and texts to the female member that I had suspected, calls of long duration, early morning, late night, and when he was supposed to be working and said he could not take my calls.

Chapter 59

M Y HUSBAND AND I WERE BOTH WOUNDED from past relationships and circumstances and had not taken the time to let
God fully heal us. Two broken people trying to fix each other never
works.

Even though our marriage did not last, I still believe that two
people who love the Lord should be able to work together and have
a successful marriage.

My husband continued to pastor the church we started together.

The following year, I moved to Florida, feeling led to go there
for a fresh start. God blessed me with a new nursing job that paid for
my moving expenses.

I started holding Bible studies in my home a few months after
I relocated. A year later, God called me to start a ministry with some
of my family members and a few people in the area who were looking
for a church home. The bishop and pastor from the church in North
Carolina where my husband and I met became my overseers. I was so
very grateful that they believed in me enough to do so.

After a couple of years, my husband reached out to me, and we
had discussions about possibly trying to reconcile. But I was skeptical
about uprooting and going back to North Carolina to be with him,
not knowing if things would be any different. Also, the ministry in

Florida was in its infancy stages, and I did not believe that God was leading me to end it. He filed for a divorce, and we were divorced four years after we separated.

The last time he and I communicated, we were still both single and ministering.

Thank God He still recycles and uses damaged goods.

I believe the latter will be greater than the former, especially since tribulation works with patience and patience with experience and experience with hope.

This is the diary of a first lady.

About the Author

WHILE HER MOTHER WENT THROUGH NURSING SCHOOL and worked part-time cleaning homes, the author, as a young child, began to walk in her God-given gifts of help and mercy as she helped her mother raise her two younger brothers and a sister. While other children her age were out playing, she was washing diapers, making bottles, and taking care of siblings. Her mother often referred to her as their second mother.

At the age of five, she became fascinated with her mother's class nursing picture that sat on the end table. Everyone looked so professional, dressed in their starched white uniforms, hats, and shoes. She began to feel the call in her life to become a nurse as well.

When the author was eight years old, her mother relocated with her children from Cleveland, Ohio, to McDowell, West Virginia, where her parents lived, fleeing domestic violence, poverty, and other insecurities.

Once under the supervision of their grandparents, the author began to learn about the Lord as her devout Christian grandmother, later joined by her grandfather, faithfully took her and her siblings to church. However, she did not fully surrender her life to the Lord until much later in life.

She eventually fell in love with Jesus, got married for the third time, started a church with her husband, and became a first lady. During this season of her life, she experienced the dilemma of the first becoming the last.

She completed Bible college and has been a minister of the gospel for over twenty years.

She followed her passion and calling by earning a nursing degree and has been a registered nurse for thirty-five years.

She is the mother of three beloved children and three grandchildren.

www.ingramcontent.com/pod-product-compliance
Lightning Source LLC
Chambersburg PA
CBHW031318160726
47993CB00001B/453